Outline Studies in
ACTS

Outline Studies in
ACTS

ROBERT LEE

KREGEL PUBLICATIONS
Grand Rapids, Michigan 49501

Outline Studies in Acts by Robert Lee. Copyright © 1987 by Kregel Publications, a division of Kregel, Inc. All rights reserved.

Library of Congress Cataloging-in-Publication Data

Lee, Robert, 1872-1956.
 Outline Studies in Acts.

 Reprint. Originally published: The Outlined Acts. London: Pickering & Inglis, 1931.
 1. Bible N.T. Acts—Sermons—Outlines, syllabi, etc.
I. Title.
BS2625.L397 1987   251'.02   87-3083
ISBN 0-8254-3141-7

1 2 3 4 5 Printing/Year 91 90 89 88 87

Printed in the United States of America

CONTENTS

SECTION 1   THE LORD AT WORK IN JERUSALEM
ACTS 1:1—7:60

6   Contents

SECTION 2   THE LORD AT WORK IN JUDEA AND SAMARIA

ACTS 8—9

SECTION 3   THE LORD AT WORK IN UTTERMOST PARTS

ACTS 10:1—28:31

Contents 7

8 Contents

PUBLISHER'S PREFACE

Personal and group Bible studies are becoming very popular. It is encouraging to know that Christians — and non-Christians — are taking seriously the study of God's Word. And a good way to get a better understanding of the Bible is to study it book by book!

The *Robert Lee Outline Studies Series* is an excellent study guide to help you discover various books of the Bible. They will help you obtain a better knowledge of God's Word and give you direction in applying it to your life. The expositional outlines, practical notes and illustrations give insights into each passage studied. Preachers and teachers will also find these outlines helpful in their sermon and lesson preparation.

The abbreviations used refer to the following translations: A.V. = Authorized or King James Version; C. & H. = Conybeare and Howson; J. N. D. = Darby's New Testament; M. = Moffatt's translation; R. = *Rotherham's Emphasized Bible*; R.V. = Revised Version; 20 C. = *Twentieth Century New Testament*; W. = Weymouth's *New Testament in Modern Speech*; and Y. = Young's translation.

BIRD'S-EYE VIEW OF ACTS

KEY VERSE. Chapter 1, verse 8, is the key to the analysis. The entire book records the fulfilment of the prophecy of 1. 8, showing how the establishment of the Christian faith began in Jerusalem, spread " to all Judea and Samaria," and eventually reached " the uttermost part of the earth." The book opens with the preaching of the Gospel in Jerusalem, the great ecclesiastical centre of the Jewish nation, and closes with the preaching of the blessed Evangel in Rome, the great centre of the world's power.

MESSAGE. The first verse of the book is the key to its message. The entire book shows how the work Jesus " began " to do (1. 1) as recorded in the Gospels, was, and is, continued by Him through the Holy Spirit. This book gives prominence to the Lord Jesus. He is *the* Worker.

PROMINENT PERSONALITIES. The Lord Jesus, and the Holy Spirit, usually work through human instrumentality. Though many men and women appear on the canvas, the two prominent personages in Acts are—

> (1) PETER, in the first great section of the book, 1. 1 to 9. 43.
> (2) PAUL, in the rest of the book, 10. 1 to end.

THE AUTHOR. Luke, the writer of the third Gospel.

PLACE AND DATE. Written from Rome, about A.D. 63.

PERIOD COVERED. From A.D. 30 to 63.

CONNECTION WITH OTHER BOOKS. Acts is a continuation to the Gospel of Luke, but might also be called a sequel to all the Gospels. Verse 3 refers to the Resurrection (see end of Matthew); verses 9, 10 describe the Ascension (see Mark); verses 7, 8 record the Promise of the Spirit (see Luke); while verse 11 points to the Second Coming, and links with the end of John.

ANALYSIS.

THE LORD AT WORK
IN JERUSALEM

ACTS 1—7

From the ascension of our Lord to the death of Stephen
(A.D. 30-37). The church founded and her Jewish period
of witness.

1. The Ascension of our Lord (1:1-11)
2. Waiting for the Spirit (1:12-14)
3. Appointment of an Apostle (1:15-26)
4. Pentecost, the advent of the third person of
   the Holy Trinity (2:1-47)
5. Opposition to the Church. The Lame Man
   Healed (3:1-26)
6. The First Persecution (4:1-37)
7. Severe Judgments (5:1-42)
8. Administration, or the Appointment of Deacons
   (6:1-15)
9. Stephen's address and martyrdom (7:1-60)

WORDS AND DEEDS

These verses give the true viewpoint of the message of this book—that is, that Acts forms a sequel to Luke; the latter telling what Jesus began to do, this book what He continued to do and teach from the Throne through others.

I. DOING AND LIVING

"Jesus began...to do." For thirty years our Lord lived the life before He sought to teach others the kind of life to live. Let us follow His example.

II. TEACHING AFTER LIVING

"And teach." Service for others is imperative. We must pass on to others the light God has given to us.

III. BOTH LIVING AND TEACHING

Our Lord both lived and taught. God has joined living and working together, and they must not be separated for long.

IV. THE ONE WHO LIVED AND TAUGHT

The message of the Acts is the Lord Jesus, THE Worker. This is the true viewpoint for the study of this book.

V. UNCEASING ACTIVITY

"He began to do and teach," but has never ended, for He ever lives. How can there be a complete biography of a person who still lives ?

Theophilus. This Greek name combines the name of God and love. Certainly he was "a lover of God " (the meaning of the word). His title, " Most Excellent," in Luke 1. 3, indicates that he was a person of rank. How cheering to see one in so high a station of life interested in Divine things.

Rechristen the Book? Its title has been the subject of many discussions. Could it not be renamed, " The Acts of the Risen, Ascended, and Glorified Lord ? " Luke records His life in the flesh ; the Acts records His life in the Spirit.

Acts an Unfinished Book. This is the only unfinished book in the Bible. Observe how abruptly it closes. How else could it close ? How can there be a complete account of His life seeing He ever liveth and works ? Henry Ward Beecher undertook to write a life of Christ. He was engaged upon it when his last fatal illness seized him. A visitor expressed the hope that he might be spared to finish the " Life of Christ." " *Finish* the ' Life of Christ,' " murmured Beecher. " Finish the ' *Life of Christ* ! ' Who can finish the ' Life of Christ,' for He lives ! "

Nothing to Unlearn. The 20 C. reads : " Dealt with all that Jesus did and taught *from the very first.*" Would any other preacher care for ALL his earthly teaching to be taken down ? Unlike us, our Lord had nothing to unle rn, nothing to undo or regret. His teaching was never immature. Verse 2 is the explanation. " He, *through the Holy Ghost,* had given commandments." Remarkable sentence ! Nowhere else are the commands of the Risen Saviour said to have been given thus.

THE PROOF OF LIFE

" Alive...by many infallible proofs "

Salvation includes " passing from death unto life." If we have been " quickened who were dead in trespasses and sins," then " many infallible proofs " will bear witness that we are truly alive.

I. EMPTY SEPULCHRES .. .. Matthew 28. 6
The world is the place for the spiritually dead, not for the living. Can an angel point to an empty tomb in your life, an empty seat in the world ?

II. DISCARDED GARMENTS .. .. John 20. 7
Typical of evil habits, the shroud of a dead soul, thrown off when the soul is quickened by God's Spirit.

III. SPIRIT OF FORGIVENESS .. .. Mark 16. 7
" And Peter." The same beautiful spirit of forgiveness in us is a proof of the possession of life eternal.

IV. MEETING WITH HIS OWN .. Matthew 28. 7
" He goeth before you into Galilee." An ardent longing to meet with God's people is another sign, for " birds of a feather flock together."

V. LIVING FOR OTHERS .. .. Luke 24. 27
Christ's mission during the forty days was for the blessing of others.

VI. HOLY CONVERSATION .. .. .. Acts 1. 3
A doctor looks at the tongue to ascertain the physical condition. The measure of delight in speaking of heavenly things will mark one's spiritual condition.

A Spiritual Resurrection. Salvation includes a spiritual as well as a literal resurrection.

" Buried with Christ, and raised with Him too,
What is there left for me to do ?
Surely to cease from struggle and strife,
Simply to walk in newness of life."

If we are really " alive " there will be many infallible proofs.

Where the Dead Live. It was an Irishman who defined a cemetery as a " place where the dead live." The world is indeed a place where those spiritually dead live. To many life itself is a death before its time. They that live in pleasure are dead while they live (1 Tim. 5. 6).

Passing from Death Unto Life (John 5. 24). What a strange journey is this ! But all who, truly penitent, trust the Saviour, take that journey. " *Appearing to them at intervals,*" so reads Weymouth of verse 3.

WITNESSING

" Ye shall be witnesses unto Me ; " and for this there are five essential qualifications—

I. PERSONAL KNOWLEDGE OF CHRIST
It is essential that a witness has personal experience and knowledge of the facts to which he testifies.

II. PERSONAL CONSISTENCY
There is a life to live as well as a story to tell. The witness of the life is most powerful.

III. PERSONAL COURAGE
Real courage is required to speak the truth under all circumstances.

IV. PERSONAL PATIENCE
Patience is a grace for which special grace is given.

V. PERSONAL POWER
Divine equipment, the clothing of the individual by the Holy Spirit.

They Were Not to Depart from Jerusalem. Just what they might have done, seeing how unkindly it had treated their Lord.

They had to Work, and Not Peer into the Future. Surely that is the meaning of verses 6 and 7. Evidently He had not touched upon this during the Forty Days. By these verses He taught that their great work was to witness for Christ. They were to be absorbed not in *counting*, but in witnessing ; not dates, but service.

Waiting. No command is given to wait for conversion or salvation from sin—that is always a present duty, binding upon every sinner. But they had to wait for the Holy Spirit.

Praying for the Spirit. Sometimes we are told that in spite of Luke 11. 13, we are not now to pray for the Holy Spirit because He is already here. But when the Holy Spirit came to earth He did not leave Heaven. We must not forget He is omnipresent.

True Witnessing. Verse 8. (1) *Its central theme*, " Me." (2) *Its expanding sphere* : (a) " Jerusalem " (our homes) ; (b) " Judaea " (our townsfolk) ; (c) " Samaria," our enemies and countrymen ; (d) " uttermost parts," the wide world. (3) *Its Only Source*, " The Holy Spirit." (4) *Its unfailing secret*, " the power of the Holy Spirit."

GOD'S POSTMEN

The Lord's witnesses have been called God's postmen

I. COMPARISONS.   God's witness is like a postman because :
1. **He Wears the King's Uniform.**
   (*a*) The garment of imputed righteousness.
       (Rom. 4. 6).
   (*b*) The livery of love (John 13. 34, 35).
2. **The Business of his Life is Carrying Messages to Others.**
   As country postmen, we may have other trades, but
   this is THE vocation.

II. CONTRASTS.   God's witness is unlike a postman because :
1. **He Knows the Message he is Delivering,** while a postman
   does not.   Though many of old did not know this
   fully (see 1 Peter 1. 11).
2. **He is Expected to be a Living Example of the Message**
   he is delivering.   This is the meaning of a witness.
   Unless we are, our message will fall flat.
3. **He is Dependent upon the Grace and Presence of the**
   Sender, without which he is helpless.
4. **He is Never Off Duty.**
5. **Success is Dependent upon his Touch of Love.**   This is
   the real secret of success, as it gives—
   (*a*) *Gentleness* to the Christian worker.   The love
       touch is a gentle touch.
   (*b*) *Sympathy.*   Love is wonderfully sympathetic, re-
       flecting His example.   " Touched with the feelings
       of our infirmities.
   (*c*) *Self-forgetfulness.*   Love is sacrificial in its opera-
       tion.
   (*d*) *Persistence.*   Love alone perseveres over all
       difficulties.

The Touch of Love.   " Thou hast loved my soul from the pit of cur-
ruption " (Isa. 38. 17, R.V., *margin*) is one of the gems of the Bible.   Love
is the great and mighty lever.   " Love lifted me " we sing.   Love is the

Secret of the Popularity of the Gospel.   " How is it that your books sell
better than mine ? " inquired a scientist of a writer of popular fiction.
" Because there is love in them," was the significant reply.   John 3. 16
is THE secret of the wonderful attraction of the Gospel.

SPIRITUAL DYNAMICS

I. SAVING DYNAMIC   ..   ..   ..   Rom. 1. 16
     Christ's **Gospel** is the great Saving Dynamic.

II. HEALING DYNAMIC   ..   ..   ..   Acts 4. 7
     Christ's **Name** is the great Healing Dynamic.

III. UPHOLDING DYNAMIC ..   ..   ..   Heb. 1. 3
     Christ's **Word** is the great Upholding Dynamic.

IV. PROPELLING DYNAMIC   ..   ..   Acts 1. 8
     Christ's **Spirit** is the great Propelling Dynamic
         (see Ezek. 36. 27).

V. OPTIMISTIC DYNAMIC   ..   ..   Rom. 15. 13
     Christ's **Spirit** is the great Optimistic Dynamic.
     Note : " Hope through the *power* of the Holy
         Spirit.

VI. CONVINCING DYNAMIC   ..   ..   Acts 3. 12
     Christ's **Life** expressed in our heart and life in
     Holiness is the great Convincing Dynamic.

VII. MORAL DYNAMIC   ..   1 Cor. 15 43 ; Phil 3. 10
     Christ's **Resurrection** is the great Moral Dynamic.
     Note : The *power* of His resurrection.

Dynamite. When the inventor of a new and powerful explosive desired a name, he took the Greek *dunamis*, rendered " power " in our English Bible, and gave it its English dress—hence dynamite. This lends emphasis to our word " power." Power is one of the great needs of the day. If we are the Lord's, some great Bible dynamics are ours, as above.

Power in His Name. Not only can we say, " How *sweet* the Name of Jesus sounds," but, How *powerful* is that Name.

Power of the Holy Spirit. The Holy Ghost is God's dynamite. The lack of that power is very manifest these days. Someone has quaintly remarked that the first century produced *missionary* Christians, but succeeding centuries have produced *omissionary* Christians.

THE PRIMITIVE UP LOOK

" This same Jesus shall so come in like manner as ye have seen Him go." His Ascension was—

I. LITERAL
His return will be literal and not spiritual.

II. BODILY
As His resurrection body was " flesh," so shall be His body in the Second Advent.

III. PARTLY SECRET
So will be the first stage of His coming in the air (1 Thess. 4. 17). His return to the earth to be seen by all will be separated from this by a slight interval (Zech. 14. 4).

IV. WITH CLOUDS
So will be His return (Rev. 1. 7), and that which once hid Him will in that day reveal Him.

V. IN OPEN DAY
When He returns it will be day in some parts of the world (Matt. 24. 40, 41) and night in others (Matt. 24. 43 with 25. 6). " Closing beneath Him hid Him from their sight " (verse 9, W.).

VI. WITH A SHOUT
And so will He descend (Psa. 47. 5 ; 1 Thess. 4. 16).

VII. FROM MOUNT OF OLIVES
(Acts 1. 12). Where He will return (Zech. 14. 4).

VIII. BEFORE THE TRIBULATION
Before the fall of Jerusalem. And His return to the air will be before the Great Tribulation.

Brevity. What amazing brevity ! The stupendous fact of the Ascension is told in one verse (9), and in a single graphic sentence (verse 10, " Why stand ye gazing up into Heaven ? ") is indicated the primitive uplook.

" **Out of their sight** " (verse 9), but not out of their reach. It was only when He was hidden from them that the disciples realised how truly present He was with them. Blessed paradox ! He went away that He might be always with them.

" **Why stand ye gazing ?** " Because they were angels and not men they asked " Why," not knowing experimentally a human being's emotions. Angels, in consequence, make but poor gospellers.

Who Saw Him Last ? As the Lord's own dear ones were the last to see Him, so they will be the first to see Him at His Coming.

Great Facts are spoken of in these first eleven verses. Note the following and find out others : (1) Christ's Life, 1 ; (2) Death, 3 ; (3) Resurrection, 3 ; (4) Kingdom, 3, 6, 7 ; (5) Spirit, 4, 5, 8 ; (6) Ascension, 9-11 ; (7) Second Advent, 11 . Covering a period of at least 3000 years, the present dispensation and the Millennium.

THEIR OWN COMPANY

Like draws to like in time and in eternity

I. DISCIPLES　　　To Own Company, ..　　　Acts 4. 23

Not at home with the company in jail, or
before the Sanhedrin, they were at home
with fellow-believers.

II. ABRAHAM　　　To His People,　　..　　　Gen 25. 8

This means much more than " he died."
" **Gathered to,**" a phrase only used in
earlier O.T. books, and only in reference
to a few : Abraham, Isaac, Moses, Aaron,
and one of a whole congregation (Judges
2. 10). " **His people,**" not his ungodly
relatives, but great men, such as Adam,
Seth, Noah, etc. Now no longer a solitary
pilgrim. Death sets the solitary in families.

III. JUDAS　　　..　　To His Own Place,　　　Acts 1. 25

The life of Judas is one of the tragedies of
history. He must have been a man of
ability, for the Lord made him treasurer
and secretary. He fell a victim to covetous-
ness, and began to pilfer, to appropriate
money from the bag for his own use. He is
called by John " a thief." During his life
he ever considered himself as one of the
company, yet never was he really one of
them. Note, he never called Jesus, Lord,
but Master, for he never really understood
Him. Hell was his before he went there—
he possessed it and carried it about with him.

Mary. The last seen of Mary, the mother of Jesus, is at a prayer meeting
(Acts 1. 14).

Ten Days' Prayer Meeting. This " upper room " (verse 13) and " one
place " (2. 1) was where the Passover had been kept (Luke 22. 12). It
lasted for ten days (see 3. 5 and 2. 1), and the Eleven Apostles, certain
women, the brothers of Jesus, who now believed (John 7. 5) were present
with the others.

Why were they Waiting ? " The promise of the Father " (verses 4, 5).
This was then fulfilled, and we do not *wait* now, but take.

The New Apostle (21-26). Note qualifications (21-22). He was " *put
forward,*" not " *appointed* " (23). They did not ask God to choose, but to
show them whom He had chosen. See " *hast,*" not " *wilt.*" " *Part,*" *i.e.,*
the place forfeited by Judas.

The Lot (verse 26). This is the last time lots were cast. With the
descent of the Holy Spirit there is now no need of such an expedient to
discover the will of God.

THE WIND OF GOD

Like the wind, the Holy Spirit is—

I. INVISIBLE
Only discoverable by results.

II. MYSTERIOUS
It is air in motion. It rushes past, but leaves no gap. Though we know much concerning its nature and laws, there is still much mystery about it.

III. SOVEREIGN
Beyond human control.

IV. EVERYWHERE
Pervading everything.

V. FORMED BY HEAT AND COLD
The Holy Spirit is here because of glowing heat (warmth of the heart of God) and icy cold (a world wrapped in the icy grip of spiritual death).

VI. LIFE-GIVING
The ministry of the wind in the world is indispensable. Without it no life could exist.

VII. PURIFYING
Cleansing the atmosphere of unwholesome vapours.

Napoleon. The great Napoleon is declared to have said a little while before his death : " When I am gone, my spirit will return to France to throb with ceaseless life in new revolutions." He died. His prediction seemed to be a true one. His military genius, the inspiration of his wonderful personality, was felt for a generation in European politics. But his influence has waned year by year as inevitably as the echo dies away when the voice that woke it has been silenced.

A Greater than He. When Another was near death, He said, " When I am gone My Spirit will return. Nay, further, My death is necessary. For it is expedient for you that I go away." He ascended up on high, and sat down on the right hand of the Majesty on high ; and that action was followed by another—" the Holy Spirit sat upon each of them." The Christ of God sat upon His Father's throne ; the Spirit of God sat upon His Father's children.

A Difference. But here lies a great difference. Napoleon's spirit was a mere influence ; the Spirit of Jesus Christ was and is a Person, a thinking, intelligent, active Personality. And the influence of that wondrous Personality has never waned.

A Sound. Observe, what filled the house was not agitated air or wind, but " a sound as of wind." This language implies that there was no rush of atmosphere that moved a hair, but only such a *sound* as is made by a tempest.

SUDDENLY

I. SUDDEN CONVERSION .. .. .. Acts 9. 3

Though Saul's conversion was sudden at the crisis, yet note the steps that lead to it (see first footnote).

1. Contact with Jesus Christ.

Preb. Webb Peploe held a conviction that the rich young ruler of Matthew 19. 16 was Saul of Tarsus. This may or may not be true, but no doubt Saul had heard of the Lord Jesus, and probably had seen Him too.

2. Contact with the First Christian Martyr (Acts 7. 58).

Was Saul so affected by Stephen's martyrdom that he was seeking to stifle conviction by increased activity in seeking out and imprisoning Christians ?

3. Contact with the Risen Lord Jesus (Acts 9. 3).

When he discovered two remarkable facts :
(a) That He was alive.
(b) That He had mysterious union with His people.

II. SUDDEN ENDUEMENT .. .. .. Acts 2. 2

Note also the steps that lead to this :
1. **They Became Believers.**
2. **Then Disciples,** *i.e.*, learners.
3. **They were Obedient.**
4. **And Patient.**
5. **United in Heart and Purpose.** (Acts 1. 14).

Previous Causes. "That blow has done it," exclaimed spectators watching the demolition of old St. Paul's, after the Great Fire of London, as the stubborn wall was seen at last to totter and fall. "You are wrong," said Sir Christopher Wren, "for every blow of the battering ram contributed its part." Many things happen suddenly in nature that can be traced as the result of previous causes, as a thunderstorm (slow gathering of electricity), a flood (slow gathering of rain), or a fall of a cliff (undermining for years).

The Manifestation of the Spirit. Note (1) The Day, (2) The Company, (3) The Place, (4) The Sound, (5) The Light, (6) The Power, (7) The Enduement, and distinguish between the Baptism and the Filling of the Holy Spirit, the former once for all, the latter oft repeated.

Three Symbols of the Holy Spirit. (1) The Wind, the *mystery* of the Church ; (2) The Fire, the *individual* possession; and (3) The Tongues, the *universal* scope of His power.

DIVINE INTOXICATION

" Others mocking said, These men are full of new wine,"
" brim full " (W.).   Indulgence in wine leads to :

I. TRANSFORMATION OF CHARACTER
Wine always debases character, but the Holy Spirit,
the New Wine of the Kingdom, changes character
for the better.

II. OBLITERATION OF TROUBLE
Worldly men fly to alcohol to drown their troubles,
but it only adds to them.   The best helper and
surest method of being lifted above sorrow is the
fulness of the Holy Spirit.

III. A CHANGED WALK
As intoxicants alter the gait for the worse, the Spirit
infilling gives the power to " walk in newness of
life."

IV. ALTERATION OF SPEECH
Strong drink loosens many tongues, but the Holy
Spirit enables speech to be seasoned as with salt.

V. NERVES FOR GREAT ENCOUNTERS
For a difficult task a worldling may fly to the stimu-
lation of strong drink as a tonic to brace his nerves.
But this kind of stimulant is only temporary, as
well as leaving an adverse effect afterwards.   But
the best preparation is the fulness of the Holy
Spirit, enabling a believer to be " strong in the
grace that is in Christ Jesus."

Materialistic Explanation.   " Full of new wine."   This was said partly
in jest, and partly as an explanation of this strange phenomenon.   How
ready the world is with materialistic explanations.

Nearer the Truth.   In their jest they were nearer the truth than they
imagined.   They *were* intoxicated, but with the wine of the Kingdom.
Those who have had an overwhelming manifestation of the Spirit declare
that their feelings have been similar in some respects to an intoxicated
person—they have reeled to and fro, and have been filled with ecstasy
and delight.

" **In One Place** " (verse 1).   Probably in the Court of the Temple.

THE NAME

Calling upon the Name of the Lord will bring salvation in the experience of anyone who is :

I. UNSAVED

Salvation for a call and instantly, because the Lord is—
1. **Not far off,** so even a whisper is heard by Him.
2. **Not unwilling,** but eager to save.
3. **Not indifferent,** but intensely interested in the welfare of every soul.

II. UNDELIVERED

To be saved means more than pardon and justification. It includes deliverance from the power of sin.

III. TEMPTED

" Breathe that Holy Name in prayer."

IV. HARASSED

No trouble is too slight for Him to be interested in it.

The Name. Mentioned at least thirty-three times in this book. See 2. 21, 38 ; 3. 6, 16 ; 4. 10, 12, 17, 18, 30 ; 5. 28, 40, 41 ; 8. 12, 16 ; 9. 15, 16, 21 ; 10. 43, 48, etc., etc.

Power of the Name. That " Name " is not only sweet, but powerful, provided the one who mentions that Name is right with God (see Acts 19. 13). It must not be used superstitiously, but reverently and in faith. In an address given at King's Hall, Holborn, in 1910, S. D. Gordon passed on a record of deliverance he had heard a fortnight before. An Arab woman in Algiers had been won for Christ. She had been a Mohammedan. Her family did their best to sway her from her new faith. They coaxed, pleaded, argued, threatened, but in vain. Then they did what is characteristic of that people—they concocted a poison, very simple, very deadly, and put it secretly in her food. When she had eaten the meal, very quickly she felt the poison working, and she knew she was doomed to die. Greatly startled and distressed, she knew not what to do. She commenced to repeat the Name, the great Name. She could not repeat it aloud, but to herself. For two or three days that went on, and the poison gradually receded from her body and blood. The family watched her with strange eyes. She herself in telling the story, said : "I felt as though each time I said that Name there was like a wave of life, and in between like a wave of death." The conflict went on, but victory was given.

PRICKED HEARTS

The preacher who wants to prick heart and conscience MUST be:

I. POWERFUL

And this power only comes with the fulness of the Holy Spirit.

II. SCRIPTURAL

Expository preaching in the best sense of the word.

III. GLORIFYING CHRIST

Setting Him forth as the Risen and Glorified One.

IV. CLEAR IN ENUNCIATION

He " LIFTED UP his voice " (2. 4).

V. PERSONAL

" YE men of Judaea " (2. 14).

Plenty of Points. There must have been plenty of *points* in Peter's sermon, for we read that 3000 were pricked in their hearts in spite of thick armour of prejudice.

Joel. The book of the Prophet Joel was one of the portions arranged to be read in the Synagogues that day, hence the aptness of Philip's reference (2. 16).

God's Will and Man's Responsibility. Note verse 23. The murderers of Christ were acting in fulfilment of the Divine decree, and yet their deeds were really and absolutely their own.

" Which ye now see " (verse 33). Evidently the symbol seems to have sat and remained upon each head for some time.

A Model Sermon. Peter's address is a model of what a good address should be, and might be analysed as follows : 1, AN INTRODUCTION (14-21). He (a) *defends* the disciples (14, 15) and (b) *quotes* the prophecy of Joel (2. 28-32), which he declares is here fulfilled (16-21). 2, A DECLARATION (22-35) of the Resurrection of Jesus Christ. A fact which (a) *he proclaims* (22-24); (b) *has been predicted* (25-31) ; (c) *many witnessed*; and (d) *he now proves* (33-35). 3, A CALL (36-41) to (a) *penitence* and (b) *trust*, directed first to Israel, but also to all.

BEING SAVED

" Those that were being saved " (47, R.V.). They were :

I. **CONVICTED** .. .. verse 37

II. **CONVERTED** .. .. ,, 38

III. **OBEDIENT** .. .. ,, 41
    In their reception of the Word.
    In their witness to the world in baptism.

IV. **STEADFAST** .. .. ,, 42

V. **INCORPORATED** .. .. ,, 42
    So large an influx of new members could easily have
    swamped the Assembly, but this verse shows how
    beautifully the new converts were incorporated into
    the community. See third note below.

VI. **DEVOTED** .. .. verse 43

VII. **UNSELFISH** .. .. verses 44, 45

VIII. **RADIANT** 46, 47
    1. **Single in Purpose** .. .. verse 46
    2. **Individual Gladness** .. .. ,, 46
    3. **United Praise** .. .. ,, 47
    4. **Influential in the World** .. .. ,, 47
    5. **Successful in Ministry** .. .. ,, 47

A.V. and R.V. Note the different renderings of verse 47.
    (1) " And the Lord added to the Church daily such as *should be
    saved.*" The A.V. rendering suggesting *salvation as a future
    blessing*, of course in the light of Romans 13. 11.
    (2) " The Lord added to them day by day those that were being
    saved " (R.V.), or as Young : "And the Lord was adding those
    being saved every day to the assembly." Suggesting *salvation
    as a process*, going on all through the course of a man's life.
    Both views are correct.

Something of Pentecost Daily. "The thought that every week there
is something of Pentecost going on in the earth has been unspeakably
sweet to me. What if the Lord's people were no more than half-a-million,
I see that to keep up that number there must be about two hundred souls
saved every week. How busy is the Spirit. How God loves the world
still " (Andrew Bonar).

A Pure Church Means an Increasing Church. The primitive assembly
was noted for its purity, simplicity, and steadfastness in four things :
(1) *Doctrine* comes first. What ignorance there is to-day of even the most
elementary facts of our Christian faith. (2) *Fellowship*, assisting one
another in material as well as in spiritual matters. (3) *Breaking of Bread*,
the original simple form of the Lord's Supper. (4) *Prayers*, practical
and habitual devotion.

The Lord Added (47), and He alone can add. How many to-day are
added to some local Church by priest or minister, but have not been
added to the Church, and are not therefore " added to the Lord " (5. 14).

AT THE BEAUTIFUL GATE

In this story we have an illustration of our helplessness and the steps taken to meet that need.

I. ARRESTING ATTENTION .. .. .. verse 4

" Look on us," suggesting that his eyes were wandering, and that he was looking and speaking mechanically as life-long beggars are wont to do. This is the first thing to do in saving souls.

II. REKINDLING HOPE .. .. verse 5

All without hope are not hopeless, and this man's expectation was aroused, though it only rose to his physical need. The apostles were anxious to meet an even deeper need.

III. RECEIVING STRENGTH .. .. .. verse 7

Peter was not ashamed to take the lame beggar by the hand in a grasp of friendliness and help. How powerful is the personal touch in individual dealing with souls.

IV. PERFECT HEALING .. .. .. verses 8, 16

He walked right away, though he had never walked. He did not have to learn to walk, and he did not begin by crawling or creeping.

V. GRATITUDE TO GOD .. .. verse 8

Went straight into the Temple. To say we are healed and yet have no love for the house of prayer is a contradiction.

VI. AFFECTION FOR GOD'S SERVANTS .. .. verse 11

" **Were going up** " (R. and R.V.). " Ninth hour," 3 p.m. It was their habit. Private prayer should be a preparation for public prayer.

Beautiful Gate. One of the wonders of the world. It was of beaten brass in the form of a vine, and had been made in Greece, purchased by Herod, and floated across the sea. It took six men to open and close. When the morning sun struck it, it shone like a wall of gold. No one that had any ailment or defilement might pass it (Lev. 21. 16).

Opposites Agreeing. Peter the Impulsive and John the Contemplative are here seen together. One was able to supply what the other lacked.

" **Peter said.** " As was in keeping with their characters, Peter took speech, while John stood by assenting.

No Apologies for Poverty. A slight change will be noticed between the A.V. and R.V. In A.V. we detect a slight apologetic tone ; in the R.V. it disappears. " Silver and gold have I none, but what I have that give I." Not " such as I have," as if it was inferior to money. Peter was not apologising for the smallness of his possession, but magnifying the greatness of what he had. The expression used indicated that he possessed something more precious than gold. There is no need to apologise for poverty. Poverty is no bar to usefulness. It is the men without silver and gold who have always given the world most.

" **Fastening his eyes upon him.** " This is characteristic of our faith, which fastens its eyes on the sick and suffering.

PRESENT SALVATION

Blessing, that comes in turning us from our iniquities, is shown by its present and practical power in :

I. BREAKING THE DEADLY SPELL

A traveller in an African forest heard shrieking. He discovered that a large snake had caught the eye of a poor animal, and, apparently mesmerised, it was slowly walking toward the reptile, though uttering cries of alarm. The traveller broke the fatal spell. What an awful spell sin has thrown over the natural man. The Lord Jesus can break it and turn us away.

II. REMOVING THE CORRUPT APPETITE

" Every man is tempted when he is drawn away of his own lust and enticed " (James 1. 14). He can take away the inward desire for sin.

III. CHANGING THE HARMFUL BIAS

In the game of bowls, each wood has a bias, *i.e.*, one end heavier than the other, hence cannot go dead straight. Our natures have the bias to evil. He can change the bias.

" **Why Marvel** ? " (verse 12). Surely it is no marvel that God should perform marvels !

" **Prince of Life** " (verse 15) signifies Author, literally Originator of life.

" **Repent** " (verse 19). If the nation had repented, not only would they have got forgiveness (vv. 29 to 32), but seasons of refreshing (*i.e.*, national restoration and blessing, verses 21 and 22) would have come, Christ Himself would have been sent back (verse 20), and the Kingdom of David would have been established.

The Lord Jesus the Worker. In verse 26 the Saviour is referred to as the worker. For Son, R.V. gives *Servant*. Having raised up His Servant, God sent Him " *first* " to Israel.

How He Blesses. 1st, in pardoning (verse 9). 2nd, in bestowing spiritual enrichment (refreshing from the presence of the Lord). 3rd, turning us away from our iniquities.

INTOLERANCE

There are different kinds of Intolerance, and there is the Intolerance of the Christian Faith, because it stands for the truth, that Salvation can only be obtained in and through the Lord Jesus Christ (verse 10).

I. AS THE DESPISED ONE
" Jesus Christ of Nazareth."

II. AS THE ATONING ONE
" Whom ye crucified."

III. AS THE VICTORIOUS ONE
" Whom God raised from the dead."

IV. AS THE SAVING ONE
" By Him doth this man stand here before you whole."

Intolerance ! What seeming intolerance we have in verse 12 ! How dogmatic ! It is a most sweeping assertion. All other religious schemes and systems are swept aside as utterly useless. See other renderings :

(1) " And there is, in no one else, salvation " (R.).

(2) " And in no other is the great salvation found, for, in fact, there is no second name under Heaven that has been given among men through which we are to be saved " (W.).

(3) " And salvation comes through no one else " (20 C.).

(4) " And there is salvation by no other " (F.F.).

Intolerance that is Intolerable. The intolerance of some people is intolerable :

1. The intolerance of the *narrow-minded religious bigot*, who refuses to see any truth except through the spectacles of his own denomination. Peter was broad, strong-minded, and charitable.

2. The intolerance of an *amateur, of a quack*. But this is the intolerance of an expert, of a specialist, of a Spirit-filled man (verse 8).

Why Intolerant ? Because it is the truth—truth proved and demonstrated by all history, ancient and modern. There is a great deal of mock charity abroad. Say they : " The Buddhist, Confucianist, Mohammedans, and others are conscientious, and are working out their own salvation ! " What ? Never ! There is only One in whom there is salvation. Christ must be everything or nothing.

" None other Lamb, none other name,
    None other hope in Heaven, or earth, or sea,
None other hiding-place from guilt and shame,
    None beside Thee ! "

Sadducees (verse 1). The position of Sadducees and Pharisees is changed in the Acts compared with the Gospels. While Christ lived the Pharisees were the soul of the opposition. After the Resurrection, the Sadducees headed the opposition. It was the Resurrection that made the difference. The Sadducees were the Materialists of that time.

Name of Contempt. In verse 10 Peter proudly takes the name of contempt, " Jesus Christ of Nazareth," and binds it as a crown about his brow.

" **Given** " (verse 12). Salvation is a gift to be received.

BOLDNESS

I. ITS IDENTITY .. .. verse 13

Not brazenness, impudence, nor insolence. The disciples did not cheek their captors. Insolence never does the least bit of good.

II. ITS SUBJECTS .. .. verse 13

1. **Peter,** whose courage had oozed out less than two months before at the prick of a servant maid's tongue.
2. **John,** the gentle, winsome, calm, and collected individual.
3. **The Healed Man,** once a helpless cripple (4. 10).

III. ITS SECRET .. .. verse 13

Not produced by scholarship. "They had been with Jesus."

IV. ITS SPHERE

1. **In Approaching God** (Eph. 3. 12 ; Heb. 4. 16).
2. **In Dwelling with God** (Heb. 10. 19).
3. **In Standing before God** (1 John 4. 17).
4. **In Speaking for God** (Eph. 6. 20).

V. ITS CONDITIONS

1. **Begins** with Justification (Prov. 28. 1).
2. **Increases** when filled by the Holy Spirit (Acts 4. 8, 31).
3. **Sustained** by the Lord's presence (Heb. 13. 6).
4. **Nourished** through our prayers (Acts 4. 29). Fear would have prayed for protection, passion would have asked for retribution on enemies, but all they asked was for boldness.

VI. ITS RESULT .. .. verse 13

"They took knowledge." Happy shall we be if our demeanour recalls to spectators the ways of the Lord. Their holy boldness reminded the Judges how that other Presence had stood before them. This is a remarkable testimony to the impression the meek and gracious Sufferer had made upon His judges.

Holy Spirit and Boldness. " Our hardest rocks are just transformed mud, mud that has passed through the ministry of terrific fire. Here is Simon Peter, once as yielding as mud, having passed through the discipline of flame, firm and irresistible as rock."

Calmness. One is struck by the calmness of the apostle, so unlike his old fussy, nervy, tumultuous self, and this was due to God and His wondrous grace.

Impossible Silence. So has verse 20 been characterised,

TWO MARVELS

I. THE MARVEL OF THE MIRACLE, ch. 3. 12 ; 4. 22.

1. **No Marvel.** Surely it is no marvel that God does marvels (3. 12).
2. **Age of the Man.** The marvel of the healing lies in the age of the healed one (4. 22). Habits are fixed at 40, and it is more difficult to save one at and over that age. Easier to set a bone of the young than old.
3. **The Lesson.** Do you say, " I'm now too old ! " Read **4. 22.** Do not miss the full force of this statement. It comes at the end of the story.
4. **The Picture** presented of sinners.
   (a) Nothing repulsive in him.
   (b) He was helpless—could not walk.
   (c) It was a birth trouble.
   (d) Healed instantly.

II. THE MARVEL OF THE BOLDNESS ..   ch. 4. 13

1. **In the Temple Court** (3. 12).
   (a) In proclaiming the Deity of Jesus (4. 10, 11).
   (b) In charging home the guilt of Christ's death on the nation.
2. **Before the Sanhedrin** (4. 5).
   But their boldness before the Sanhedrin is more remarkable. Humble fishermen, bold though before seventy-one of the elite of the land, the same court and same court-house where their Lord but a short while before had been condemned !
3. **In Witnessing After Threats** (4. 33).
   Note the bold proclamation of the Resurrection of Jesus, one of the stones of stumbling to the Sadducees. As one has so truly said, " How easy it would have been for them to silence the apostle if they could have pointed to the undisturbed and occupied grave ! That would have finished the new sect at once. Is there any reason why it was not done but the one reason that it could not be done ? "

Three Results of their boldness might be noted.
1. *Praise* (4. 25-28). They did not complain, but glorified God ; and this naturally leads them on to
2. *Prayer* (4. 29, 30). Asking for protection in danger (29a) ; the provision of boldness for future witness (29b), and that the proclamation of Christ may be vindicated by results (30).
3. *Power* (4. 31). Prayer truly changes things, and after they prayed something happened. They were filled with the Holy Spirit. Note, not baptised, as that had already occurred, and once for all. But there is need for continual filling.

REPULSIONS

There are at least four things about Christianity which are both attractive but at the same time are repellent to the natural man.

I. ITS DOCTRINES

There are, of course, attractive features in Christian Doctrine, but certain truths are repellent to the natural or sinful heart. Chiefly such as :

1. The Virgin Birth.
2. The Miraculous Element.
3. Salvation by Blood and without merit.

II. ITS CLAIMS

Its claims are seemingly intolerant, *e.g.*,

1. The low gate of repentance that stands at the entrance.
2. The narrow path of self-denial is by no means pleasing.

III. ITS HOLINESS

The most effective preservative that any Christian Church can have is the consecrated, devoted, and unworldly piety of its members.

IV. ITS DISCIPLINE

" The beauty of Christ's Church is guarded by the asperity of her disciples."

Large Accessions. There had been large accessions to the Church— 3000 on Day of Pentecost, 5000 as result of healing of lame man, and many were converted day by day (4. 32). But something happened that stopped temporarily that rush—it was the judgment of Ananias and his wife.

Satan's Strategy. As his kingdom was in danger, Satan felt something must be done to avert its final overthrow. He had tried persecution, but that failed. Now he seeks to destroy it from within. Internal dangers are graver than external ones. Judgment fell swift and sudden, teaching the need of honesty and purity.

Effect was Twofold. Fear fell on the Church, leading to carefulness ; fear fell on unbelievers, showing them that to believe was no light and frivolous thing.

Repulsions. We dwell upon the attractions of our Christian faith but rarely upon its repulsions, though the latter are necessary to its purity and permanence. " Nature is an austere teacher on this point—she has given to the rose its exquisite fragrance ; but she has also armed it with thorns, so that, while the delicious odours allure, these little sentinels stand guard with their bayonets to defend the flower, which is endangered by its very beauty and sweetness."

Two Examples. BARNABAS for commendation (4. 32-37), and ANANIAS and SAPPHIRA for condemnation (4. 1-11).

CONSOLATION

Some of the qualifications for the noble ministry of consolation as seen in the life of Barnabas, who was :

I. A MAN OF FAITH 11. 24

This is the first essential in order to become a son of consolation. This is how he began his Christian life ; and the first act became the habit of his life. His activities were the activities of faith.

II. FILLED WITH THE HOLY SPIRIT 11. 24

Though not with the apostles at Pentecost. It is surmised that he was one of the converts of Pentecost. Being a Levite, he was probably performing his Temple duties.

III. A GOOD MAN 11. 24

His goodness was from God, as the result of his faith and the filling of the Holy Spirit. Good, but not faultless.

IV. HIS LIFE WAS ADJUSTED 4. 37

He was a Levite, and Levites were not supposed to hold property. This irregularity he corrected, for " having a farm, he sold it " (W.), and afterwards he had to support himself by manual labour.

V. GENEROUS AND SYMPATHETIC 9. 27

Generous, in parting with his property ; sympathetic in assisting the new convert (9. 26) who belonged to the same country (4. 36).

VI. SELF-EFFACING 13. 2, 46

Though Barnabas was the older and Saul the younger, he was not the least jealous of Saul, but at once yielded up pre-eminence.

VII. STEADFAST 13. 13

Though his nephew, Mark, cowardly forsook him, yet he continued his work. For Paul's testimony to him, 26 years later, see 1 Cor. 9. 6. He was an example of his own exhortation to steadfastness (11. 23) ; and though he disagreed with Paul, he did not abandon his God or his work.

Consolation. An ex-jockey informed me that once he was so ill that " six doctors had a *consolation* over me." Rather hard on the medical gentlemen ! No doubt their consultation over him must have been a consolation to the sick one. The apostles, in imitation of our Lord's frequent practice, bestowed upon Joseph a new name. He who was only Joseph before, is now Joseph Barnabas, *i.e.*, Joseph the Consoler. They

Continued on page 52

THE HEALING SHADOW

Conditions to be observed that our shadow might bring blessing.

I. RIGHT POSITION

A man's shadow is the result of his position with regard to the sun—its length and character depending on where he stands in relation to the shining rays. Am I right with the Sun of Righteousness ?

II. RIGHT ATTIRE.

The character of the attire has something to do with the shadow. We have to put ON Christ, as well as to put IN Christ. Note the influence of a mere look—Jesus looked on Peter and it broke his heart. Of Erskine it was said : " His looks were better than a thousand homilies."

III. RIGHT TEMPERATURE

Both an iceberg and a fire exert influence, but what a difference ! The presence of the iceberg is known long before the sailors see it—it lowers the temperature of the water and atmosphere. Am I proper, yet cold as an iceberg, or as a fire ablaze for God ?

Shadow of Value. Then the shadow of a good man is of value ! Then his presence or journey in the streets bestows boons and blessings ! Truly.

God Honouring His People. The purpose of the insertion of this incident is to show how highly esteemed the disciples were. " They that honour Me I will honour," remains for ever true.

Is this True ? But is this true, or was it only a superstitious idea ?

Not Isolated. Observe, this was so " in every street " (so R.V. and A.V. *margin*), so was not the act only of the poor and illiterate. Note " beds and couches." The " beds " were those of the well-to-do ; the " couches " were the mats or pallets of the very poor. So this was the act of rich and poor, educated and illiterate.

No Command. There is no evidence they were commanded to do this thing. Some have also stated that there is no evidence that any were healed by Peter's shadow. But what about verse 16 ?

Oriental Belief. There are to-day thousands who believe the shadow of men can bless or defile. Some Hindu sailors were having their meal, when some English visitors passed, the one casting their shadow upon the food, when the hungry sailors angrily arose and threw the food overboard.

Do you say " Rubbish ? " Not so fast, friend. (1) How is it that it is easier to speak in some churches and assemblies than others ? A difference in Spiritual atmosphere. (2) How is it that some very deaf people love to attend meetings for worship, though they cannot hear a word ? They say it is the spiritual atmosphere they enjoy. (3) How is it that the presence of some lower, whilst others raise, the spiritual atmosphere of a place ?

The Shadow of our Influence. All cast an invisible shadow, only we call it by another name—influence. It is the shadow cast by our personality, an influence which flows from us without any effort on our part. Does your shadow heal or wound, soothe or irritate, warm or chill, exalt or depress ? Consider the above outline.

THE SHADOW OF CHRIST

The previous study naturally leads us to think of some of the
blessings which come from the shadow of our Lord Jesus Christ.

I. HEALING ..   Song of Sol 2. 3, with Malachi 4. 2
> Modern Science speaks loudly in favour and support of
> the healing efficacy in light and sun-rays. There is
> healing in Him, beneath His wings.

II. SAFETY .. .. Psalm 17. 8
> " Hide me under the shadow of Thy wings." But
> observe the former part of the verse : " Keep me as
> the apple of the eye." That is the purpose of His
> shadow and the instantaneousness of His keeping.

III. COMFORT .. .. Isaiah 25. 4 ; 32. 2
> How precious are these statements.

IV. SUSTENANCE .. .. .. Song of Solomon 2. 3
> Not only shelter from the heat and safety from the
> tempest, but nourishment and refreshment for the
> soul.

V. REJOICING .. .. Psalm 63. 7

VI. GROWTH .. .. Mal. 4. 2
> " And grow up." Skilled gardeners tell us that the
> most mellow fruit is not that which has ripened in
> the full blaze of the sun, but that which lies under
> the shade of leaves that shield it from the burning
> rays.

VII. ACTIVITY .. .. Mal. 4. 2
> " And ye shall go forth." Spiritual activity.

VIII. VICTORY .. .. Mal. 4. 2
> " And ye shall tread down the wicked." Victory comes
> under His shadow.

The Shadow of Christ. If some doubt the healing efficacy of man's
shadow, none of His own dear people can ever doubt the healing there is in
the shadow of Christ because of actual personal experience.

Sitting Under His Shadow (Song of Sol. 2. 3). This statement is only
appreciated in hot scorching weather. Only then can we place a right
value on that shadow. It is a position of great privilege. No Eastern
servant would ever dare to sit in his Master's presence except commanded
by him to do so. To sit in the Master's presence and shadow means friendship of a very real character. He thus treats us as friends, and not as
servants. Sitting beneath His shadow is sitting under " an apple tree,"
and not a weeping willow, for He wipes the tears from our eyes. The
shadow of sorrow without the shadow of Christ will have a tendency to
sour us.

A Solemn Reminder. Only they who sit under His shadow now will by
and by sit with Him in His Throne.

PERMANENCY

The one condition of endurance and permanency : " If it be of God ye cannot overthrow it " (39). This is the secret of the permanency of—

I. THE CHRISTIAN CHURCH

Considering the opposition of enemies, the hindrances through the lives of adherents, one of the greatest miracles in the world to-day is the existence and strength of the Christian Church.

II. THE CHRISTIAN SALVATION

One rejoices at the conversion of a soul. One also trembles when he remembers the storm awaiting that frail barque just launched. No need to be anxious. If it be of God it cannot be overthrown.

III. THE CHRISTIAN SERVICE

None cares to labour for nothing. We like to think our service will stand, and it will, if wrought in God.

Second Persecution. The popularity of the apostles roused the enmity of the Jewish leaders. " Filled with *jealousy*," is literal rendering of the verse 17. Thus began the second great persecution. This time they put ALL the apostles in prison (verse 18). But that night (verse 19) the Lord delivered them. Often He works " at night," when He is least expected. Note the vain search (verses 22 to 25). They found them in Temple.

" Words of this Life " (verse 20). What an original description ! God's Word : 1st Describes THE life ; 2nd, Imparts THE life.

Doors Shut (verse 23). The angel not only OPENED the prison doors, but had also closed them. That is a point worth noting. In cold weather, as we pass in and out of rooms, let us be a little more considerate.

" Prince and a Saviour " (verse 31). He is a Royal Saviour—Prince in His Royalty ; Saviour in His Messiahship. " To give." He is not only the *Medium* through whom the gifts come, but also the *Dispenser* of them.

Pain of Heart (verse 33). Here pain of heart leading to hatred, whereas in Acts 2. 37, pain of heart led to repentance.

Gamaliel (verse 34). One of the great heroes of Rabbinic history. He was grandson of the great Hillel, and son of Simon who is thought to be the Simeon of Luke 2. 25. It is to his credit that he stood calm, and curbed the howling of the fanatics around him. It has been said that he was the first and only Jewish authority, who counselled abstinence from persecution. Some have imagined him to be a secret disciple. We fear this was not so. The only relic of his wisdom left, save this incident, is a prayer against Christian heretics. He lived and apparently died a Jew.

Wisdom of a Neutral Policy. There is no doubt that the neutral policy advocated here (verses 38 and 39) was truest wisdom. It is good to adopt at times this policy to-day. The way to spread error is to persecute its teachers. Error, if left alone, will often die of itself. Sometimes our duty is to oppose error.

" And Beaten Them " (verse 40). So they did not *fully* carry out the wise advice of Gamaliel.

FULNESS

To be filled with the Holy Spirit in life, character, and service will result in fulness of :

I. FAITH   ..   .. verse 5
> Both the condition of filling and one of its blessed results.

II. GRACE   ..   .. verse 8 (R.V.)
> Grace sometimes is a general term meaning :
> 1. **Gift of God.**
> 2. **Graces of the Spirit.**
> 3. **Graciousness,** *i.e.,* Sweet Winsomeness.

III. POWER   ..   .. verse 8
> Evidenced by the bold testimony given for God, and the power in which it was given.

IV. WISDOM   ..   .. verse 10
> An exhibition of this is seen in Stephen's speech. See next Study.

V. GENTLENESS   ..   .. verse 10
> Note the contrast between the raging fanatics grinding their teeth and howling around Stephen, and the calmness, tranquillity, and courtesy of Stephen.

VI. RADIANCY   ..   .. verse 15
> His glowing radiancy of countenance.

VII. VISION 7. 55, 56

VIII. FORGIVENESS 7. 60
> Reflecting the forgiving spirit of Christ.

"**Full of the Holy Ghost.**" There is something suggestive and impressive in the fact that this description comes at the close as at the beginning of the record of Stephen's work (6. 5 ; 7. 55). A competent Greek authority states that in the Greek here, " being full " implies not a sudden inspiration, but a permanent state. Thus from first to last he was filled.

Notable Fact. This is a fact worthy of our special notice. It is one thing to be filled with the Holy Spirit, quite another to be kept filled. Many lose this blessing (1) *when promoted to higher official position*; not so Stephen. (2) *In and through controversy* ; but Stephen did not. (3) *In and through suffering and persecution* ; but Stephen remained filled.

Success Embarrassing. Success here was embarrassing (verse 1). The Greek Hebrew Christians thought that in the daily ministrations their widows came worse off than Jerusalem Hebrew widows, and manifested a somewhat jealous spirit. The twelve did not stand on their dignity and refuse to listen to the Hellenists, but exhibited grace, tact, and wisdom. They admitted they might have given cause for their murmuring. They had more important work to do in ministering the Word of God and prayer, and suggested the selection of seven men.

Uncommon Qualifications for Common Tasks. Note the sort of men

Continued on page 52

STEPHEN'S SPEECH

In this chapter is given the reply of the first Christian martyr to the accusation which will be found in chapter 6. 11-14.

I. INTRODUCTION .. .. verse 2

He arrests their attention at once by repeating the honoured name of Abraham, and then begins a review of their own history, to show them that there were more important things than their Temple.

II. GOD'S MESSAGE .. .. verses 1-8, 30-34, 38

You think much of this Holy Place, but God's great messages to our nation came to Abraham and Moses long before there was any temple; yea, came to them in foreign lands.

III. THE TEMPLE, A SHADOW .. .. verses 47-49

Even when the Temple was built, God declared it was but a shadow of a much more glorious substance.

IV. ACCUSING THE ACCUSERS Verses 9, 25, 27, 35, 39, 40-43, 51-53

You think you resemble the good qualities of our fathers, whom God so favoured. You also resemble them in your baser passions.

Magnanimous. Turn again to 6. 1 to 7. Observe all the seven men selected belonged to the murmuring section. Seven men were selected from the class that thought itself unjustly treated. And the Hebrews entrusted their widows to their care. What magnanimity !

First Office-Bearers. Here we have the appointment of the first office-bearers in the Church.

Word of God Increasing. No wonder that after the exhibition of such a loving and trustful spirit we read of multiplying blessing (verse 7). " A great number of the priests " were converted.

Stephen's Success (verse 8). Intended and set apart by man for the care of widows, God thrust him out into apostolic labours. And he also beat the opponents of the Gospel in argument (verse 10).

How was Stephen's Speech Preserved for Us ? No doubt Luke got it from Paul, then known as Saul, who was listening to the speech with no friendly ear. But it made a profound impression upon him. Students of Paul's own immortal apologies will note that he moulded them after the style of Stephen.

Did Stephen Die on Calvary ? Many think verse 58 indicates that Stephen was done to death on Calvary. It was the ordinary place of execution.

Review of History. Stephen reviews the history of the nation under the following heads : 1, ABRAHAM, the father of family (2. 8). 2, JOSEPH, the saviour of his people (9. 16). 3, THE NATION in bondage in Egypt (17-36). 4, MOSES, the deliverer of the nation (37-43). 5, IN THE PROMISED LAND, Joshua, David, Solomon (44-50). From the *Tabernacle* (44) he speaks of the *Temple* (47), but leads to the *Universe* (49-50). 6, CONCLUSION (51-53).

THE STANDING CHRIST

I. SYMPATHISER
No impassioned, cast-iron Deity, with arms folded in eternal calm and impassiveness.

II. INTERCEDER
The attitude of prayerful service.

III. SUCCOURER
But Stephen was killed. Yes. Help in sorrow is sometimes better than exemption from calamities. Support in them is infinitely better.

IV. WELCOMER
Compare Heb. 10. 12. Did the risen Lord of Glory rise to welcome the first Christian martyr ?

What they Saw ? They only saw the roof of the chamber, or if the Council met in the open Court of the Temple, the blue of the Eastern sky, and the prisoner who reminded them so much of the August Prisoner, Jesus of Nazareth, they had so recently hounded to death.

What he Saw ! But a brighter light than that of the earthly sun was flashed upon Stephen's inward eye. He opened his defence with a reference to the God of Glory (7. 2), and at its close he sees the Glory of God—Jesus.

Their Passionate Hatred. Stephen's words roused them to an even wider outburst of passionate hatred.

"I See the Son of Man." Stephen recognised Him, though probably he had never seen the Lord. " *The Son of Man.*" This name, used frequently by Jesus, is seldom used by others in the Holy Book, save Daniel, and John in Revelation. The only instance of its use outside the Gospels and the Revelation is here. It is a Messianic title. It also declares the abiding manhood of Jesus—Jesus is still man as well as God the Son.

" Standing." Thirteen times is Christ spoken of in Scripture as *seated*, but only once is He spoken of as " *standing*," and that is here. The vision does not represent Him as seated in colossal calm, as Buddha with folded arms, or as those amazing Egyptian statues of the Sphinx. Oh, blessed testimony to the deathless sympathy and tenderness of the loving Saviour's heart. He starts from His seat at the call of His injured disciple. He feels the cruel blow as if it was inflicted upon Him.

Praying to Jesus. The Holy Ghost not only enabled Stephen to see the glorified Jesus, but also to pray to Him (verse 59).

Stephen's Death Meant Life to Saul. Without doubt, this scene ultimately led to Saul's conversion.

THE LORD AT WORK
IN JUDEA AND SAMARIA

ACTS 8—9

From the persecution under Saul to his conversion (A.D. 37-38). The church persecuted but spreading and the transitional period of her witness.

1. The Persecution under Saul (8:1-4)
2. The Ministry of Philip (8:5-40)
3. The Conversion of Saul (9:1-30)
4. Peter and his Ministry (9:31-43)

SCATTERED

The scattering of the disciples was the scattering of four things :

I. LIGHT
To reveal sin and drive away darkness.

II. SALT
To cleanse and purify, making much smarting in the process.

III. SEED
To produce a harvest of righteousness.

IV. FIRE
To spread the flame of Gospel zeal.

" **On that Day.**" R.V. instead of " At that time." It appears from this that on the very day of Stephen's death a fierce persecution of the Church broke out. The enemies of the Faith had tasted blood, and this appetite for blood roused by Stephen's martyrdom at once impelled them to seek for further victims.

" **All Scattered Abroad** " except the apostles. Why they remained we know not, but we admire their courage. Officers should be the last to leave the wreck. In the meantime Stephen was buried.

" **Devout Men** " (verse 2) carried the poor battered body to the burial. These were not believers, but unconverted Jews (Acts 2. 5). They evidently had been touched by his words and death. And these good, pious men resented the violence of their compatriots. Usually the victims of stoning had no funeral honours whatsoever.

" **Went Everywhere Preaching the Word** " (verse 4). Glorious ! The purpose of the enemy in scattering the first assembly of believers was to put an end to this new movement. By the blessing of God, it had the opposite effect. After all, is not this the Lord's intention for His people, instead of settling down in little companies to have a good time, and cultivate their own spiritual lives ? Of what use is light unless it shines forth to dispel the darkness ? Salt in the salt-cellar will not do unless it is scattered. Seed must be scattered else it will not take root and produce a harvest. Fire, scattered, usually dies out ; by God's blessing here it spreads the flame of Gospel blessing.

Philip. He was one of the seven of whom Stephen had been a member (64). As soon as Stephen is taken away, Philip rises up to take his place. The noble army of witnesses never wants recruits.

Man Proposes, but God——. One cannot but notice how differently things had turned out to what the apostles intended. They had destined the seven for purely secular work, and regarded preaching as their own special duty and prerogative. The Church made Philip a deacon, but the Holy Spirit made him an evangelist, and an evangelist he continued to the end of his days (Acts 21. 8).

Samaria Prepared. See John 4. 39-42. The harvest spoken of by the Lord (John 4. 35) was now being reaped. A woman did the sowing and a man reaps. But both will receive a reward (John 4. 36), and all share in the joy (Acts 8. 8).

SIMON UNMASKED

" Thou hast neither part nor lot in this matter." Thus spake one Simon (Simon the Apostle, Simon of Judas) to another Simon (Simon Magus, the magician). This, in spite of four facts.

I. A PROFESSED BELIEVER .. .. .. verse 13
He was a professed believer, but evidently his faith was worthless. The people believed because of Philip's *preaching* (2). Simon, because of the *miracles* (13). But he was not truly saved (21-23). A professor only.

II. A BAPTISED BELIEVER .. .. .. verse 13
Though a baptised believer, baptism has no sacramentarian or regenerative value, whether mixed with faith or no.

III. ACCOMPANIED A GOOD MAN .. .. verse 13
The company of a good man is to be coveted and valued. Yet Simon found that even such company is powerless to change a life independent of personal faith in a personal Saviour.

IV. DESIRED A GOOD GIFT .. .. .. verse 19
He coveted apostolic power. It is good to have high and lofty aspirations. Observe he was not so anxious to receive the Holy Spirit as the power of conferring this blessing upon others. He regarded spiritual gifts as capable of being received and exercised apart altogether from moral qualifications. What a mistake !

Startling ! How startling is Peter's fiery rebuke (verses 20 and 21). Peter's scathing sentence is the language of mingled horror and indignation. This drives us to our knees. Though a believer, instead of being filled with the Holy Spirit, he was filled with venom—" gall of bitterness ; " instead of being in Christ, he was in bondage to iniquity.

Before Philip. Philip went down to Samaria (verse 5), but someone else had been at work there before Philip—Simon Magus. He " amazed " (R.V. for " bewitched ") them (verse 9). Probably Simon was a Jew. Most of the nobility in those days had their sorcerers (Acts 13. 6 and 7). It was a time of great spiritual unrest, and in such times folk like these spring up like mushrooms. Just as to-day, some who are weary of our Christian faith are playing with Spiritualism, Buddhism, Mohammedanism, etc.

What Peter's Language Meant. It meant that Simon Magus was perishing (verse 20) ; he had no share in the Holy Ghost (21) ; his heart was wrong (verse 21) ; he was filled with venom, and was a " bundle of iniquity" (literal), as well as being in bondage to it (verse 23).

Model Preaching. Peter's faithful dealing was intended to heal, not to slay. He first urged repentance (verse 22), then prayer. Prayer is not acceptable unless the sinner comes repenting. " Perhaps." Peter had no doubt of God's willingness to forgive, but had a doubt of Simon's sincerity. Alas, Simon turned to Peter (verse 24) instead of to Peter's Lord.

A TRUE EVANGELIST

Philip is an illustration of a true evangelist. Note four things.

I. COMMISSIONED .. .. verse 26

What a startling commission! Bidden to leave his flourishing revival work in Samaria for a desert place sixty miles away, without any explanation. Why? The Lord may have done this to keep Philip from brooding despondently over Simon.

II. PROMPTLY OBEDIENT .. .. .. verses 27, 30

He did not linger to settle up any affairs, nor arrange a farewell gathering. Did not complain at brevity of notice.

III. OPENED EAR .. .. verses 26, 29

He knew the voice of the Spirit, who is the great Ally in soul-winning. Keep close to the Saviour that you may know the Spirit's voice when He speaks.

IV. SKILFUL SOUL-WINNER .. .. .. verse 30

He was skilful and tactful in personal dealing. First of all he GOT NEAR. One of the secrets of success with men and women is to get near to them. Note his ABRUPTNESS. So unlike the ordinary long-winded oriental courtesies, that it would lead the Ethiopian to look narrowly at the speaker. Finally, Philip PREACHED JESUS and His atoning death, the very marrow of the Gospel.

He Went on his Way Rejoicing (8. 39). A notable statement. That is to say, he went on with great joy in spite of the sudden disappearance of the man who had led him into liberty, a very severe test indeed. One thing, it would lead the new convert to depend more on the Lord than on the merely human instrument.

No Rejoicing Before. He had been to Jerusalem to worship, yet he did not seem to be happy. Had he been saddened by the hollowness of the religious ceremonies and worshippers there? However, he now tastes joy for the first time.

Four Joys. This Chancellor of the Exchequer learned four joys :

1. *Joy of Discovery.* Discovery of the Saviour through Philip's exposition of the Word.
2. *Joy of Possession.* Personal acceptance of the discovered Saviour.
3. *Joy of Realisation* (verse 37). He there and then entered into a knowledge of acceptance in the Beloved.
4. *Joy of Transmission.* His nation subsequently became Christian. Surely through his testimony.

" **Spirit of the Lord Caught away Philip.** " Does this mean that an impulse so strong and irresistible that it was felt to be from the Spirit of the Lord led Philip to an abrupt and immediate departure, or was he carried away bodily by the Spirit (a journey of 20 miles from Gaza to Azotus) as Elijah was caught up to Heaven ?

A JOYFUL PILGRIMAGE

Here are steps to a joyful pilgrimage.

I. AN UNSATISFIED SOUL .. .. .. verse 27

1. **He was not entirely engrossed with the affairs of this world.** Though he had *position*, holding high office in Abyssinia; *power*, being the queen's chancellor of the exchequer; and *possessions*, having money for such a long journey, yet he found time to think of God.

2. **He had discovered** that earthly greatness could not fully satisfy the soul, for he had become a Jewish proselyte.

3. **He was prepared to go to any expense** or labour to worship God. Ethiopia to Jerusalem was a long and costly journey, taking much time out of a busy life.

4. **He had discovered the emptiness of mere ceremonialism,** for he seemed to be joyless.

II. AN INQUIRING SOUL .. .. verses 28, 31, 34

1. **He read God's Word.** spending his spare hours in its study. Perhaps he had selected this lonely and unfrequented road home in order to have more quietness for study and meditation.

2. **He was not ashamed of God's Word,** or to be seen carrying and reading it. Must have been reading aloud, for silent reading is almost unknown in the East, and also Philip heard him (30).

3. **He was meek, humble, and tractable,** though high in power and authority. His modest answer to a stranger bears witness to his eagerness to learn, not being affronted at Philip's apparent curtness, nor ashamed of confessing his non-comprehension. He was not too high to be taught by a lowly man (30, 31).

III. A CONVERTED SOUL .. .. .. verses 36-38

1. **His quick response** to the Gospel message. His was an instantaneous conversion.

2. **His ready obedience** and desire for baptism.

3. **His bright testimony.** He went on his way rejoicing, and that is the last we hear of him. But years afterwards his nation became a converted one. What did he say to his Queen when he returned ? Surely he preached Christ to his own people.

THE VOICE

" Saul, Saul, why persecutest thou Me ? " Though that was all that was said, the ardent persecutor of the Christians recognised the voice, and from it learned at least three facts.

I. JESUS WAS ALIVE

The Jesus, whom he thought was dead, was alive, and the voice revealed the Lord's risen personality.

II. HIS ONENESS WITH HIS FOLLOWERS

There was a mysterious unity between the Lord and His persecuted disciples. " Why persecutest thou *Me* ? " Here for the first time he learned this truth, which afterwards he understood better and taught so well.

III. THE LORD KNEW HIM

" Why persecutest *thou* Me ? " He not only knew him and called him by name, but knew also just how he was employing his time.

Notable Conversion. The conversion of Paul is described three times with much minuteness of detail—once by Luke the historian (here in Acts 9), twice by Paul himself, later in this book. The story occupies more space than any except that of our Lord's crucifixion. Thus is shown the importance of the subject : 1st, A conversion due to the direct personal agency of our Lord. 2nd, The important part played by the convert in the moulding of the Christian Church.

" **Yet** " (verse 1). This word is significant, taking us back to the last mention of the young disciple of Gamaliel, suggesting that side by side with the extension of the Gospel under Philip the evangelist, there was a corresponding extension of persecution of the adherents of the Gospel under Saul.

Saul's Thoroughness. " **Breathing Out** " (verse 1). Persecution was his very breath. " Whose every breath was a threat of destruction " (W.). There was nothing half-and-half about Paul. Both before and after conversion, whatever he did he did with his might, putting his whole soul into everything.

His Restlessness. The High Priest exercised a kind of jurisdiction over all Jews everywhere. To him Saul went for letters to the Synagogues of Damascus, six days' journey (140 miles) from Jerusalem. It was midday (see Acts 26. 13), when most travellers would rest, especially as they were some distance from the objective. But for Saul and those with him there was no rest. He felt too eager to be about the dread business of stamping out this new religion.

Great Light. Suddenly a great light " shined round about *him* " (verse 3). Round about *Saul and not the others.* Even in that land where the beams of the midday sun are like drawn swords, this light outshone all. Whence came this great light ? Not from the sun—it came from the face of the glorified Lord. " His face did shine as the sun " (Matt. 17. 2) at His Transfiguration. " And His countenance was as the sun shineth in his strength," is a description of Him in the last book of the Bible (Rev. 1. 16).

The Voice. He heard a voice speaking in the Hebrew tongue (Acts 26. 14). *Continued on page 52*

HARD FOR THEE

" It is hard for thee to kick against the ox-goads," was the language of an ox owner, from which Saul learned that the Lord considered him as His own, and he at once realised at least four facts.

I. HE BELONGED TO CHRIST

He was the purchased possession of Another, as the Lord likened Himself to one who had purchased a young heifer at great cost, which had resisted stoutly, compelling the owner to use the sharp-pointed goad against its flanks. Saul of Tarsus would thus suddenly awaken to the fact that he had been purchased by the Blood of the Cross, and that his rightful Owner, for long years, had been seeking to make him take the appointed track. This truth revolutionised Saul's whole life.

II. CHRIST THOUGHT HIM WORTH WHILE

He learned the source of the remorse and anguish of conscience he had endured, that its strivings and uneasiness were the pricking of the great Owner's goad, seeking to bring his rebellious will into subjection.

III. CHRIST HAD A PURPOSE FOR HIM

An ox owner uses a goad.

1. To drive forward a dilatory animal.
2. To cause it to obey his will.
3. To make it tread the path marked out.

IV. IT WAS HARMFUL TO REBEL

His rage and rebellion were harmful and impotent; he was hurting himself and not the goad.

"It is Hard for Thee" (verse 5). Then the Lord appeared to Saul for Saul's sake, and not only to press into His service another preacher! He was harming and injuring himself, and the Lord wished to save him from further pain. "The way of transgressors is hard."

Tone. How one wishes it were possible in cold print to record tone as well as words. There is at times more in tone than words. In fact, frequently tone decides the meaning of words. "It is hard for thee," should be read in a gentle, loving, and appealing tone of expostulation.

Greek Proverb. It appears that this expression, "It is hard for thee to kick against the ox-goad," was a common Greek proverb of which Saul would be well acquainted.

Speech Betrayed. When the Master thus spake, His speech betrayed Him. It was said of Him during His earthly ministry that without a parable He did not speak. Now from Heaven His lips took up the wonted strain.

FIRST STEPS

In these verses we see the first steps of a famous convert.

I. BAPTISM .. .. verse 18

There was no hesitation in confessing Christ by baptism. After regaining his sight, before he broke his three days' fast (19), he was baptised.

II. CONFESSION .. .. verse 20, R.V.

He unfalteringly proclaimed the Deity of Christ right away, which fact he also proved (22).

III. CONSECRATION .. .. Between verses 21 and 22

In Gal. 1. 17, 18 he tells us himself that he went into retreat in Arabia, which must have taken place here. Probably " after many days " (23) refers to this time. His purpose would be threefold.

1. **To Take his Bearings Afresh.** He would require time to readjust his life and thoughts.

2. **To Study God's Word,** which would open up in new and wonderful vistas when studies from this new standpoint.

3. **To Commune with God** and to be taught by the Lord Himself. And thus he was prepared to be the theologian of the Christian Church, giving at least thirteen of the Epistles.

Reverence. From respect (" Sir," in verse 5) he proceeded to reverence (verse 6), thus acknowledging the Lordship of Christ. The persecutor suddenly becomes the disciple, and learning his Master's will, obeys.

Ananias. How significant to note that the Lord did not point the way of salvation Himself, but sent His servant Ananias (read verses 10 to 17). Holy and humble souls may perform a great work in thus helping those stronger in every sense than themselves and fitted for more laborious and higher positions. " Brother Saul." Ananias gave a brother's welcome.

" He preached Jesus . . . that He is the Son of God " (verse 20). Peter, whilst maintaining the Deity of Jesus, gave special prominence to His Messiahship. Paul, fresh from the vision of the glory, puts the emphasis upon His Deity. Note the R.V. The point was, not that Christ was God (a truth plainly taught by Isaiah, and acknowledged by *all* Jews), but that Jesus, the crucified Nazarene, was the Christ, and therefore God the Son. What a staggering fact this would seem to the unconverted Jews when proclaimed by the late notorious persecutor (verse 21).

Three Years' Solitude. Between verse 21 and 22 comes the 3 years in Arabia. This he refers to in Galatians 1. 17 and 18. Undoubtedly, like Moses and Elijah, he spent some time at Mount Sinai. This we judge in a peculiar phrase in Galatians 4. 25 : " For this Hagar is Mount Sinai in Arabia." This solitude was necessary. How important it is for those servants of the Lord who feel called to devote *all* their time and talents to the Lord's service to undergo a two or three years' course of special study and prayer, preferably at some Bible College or accredited Training Home.

Continued on page 52

SECRET OF INCREASE

In these verses we have some of the secrets of an increasing
Church.

I. OPPOSITION .. .. verse 29
The opposition of the world, sanctified and blessed, had
much to do with the multiplication. The embers of
the holy fire were scattered, and thus ignited others.

II. PEACE .. .. verse 31
Rest of soul and mind. There was rest from the persecutor, but that would have been of little avail if
they had not possessed rest of another kind.

III. KEEPING TRYST
One has wisely remarked : " The right use of quiet
times is a great secret of Christian living." We do
not read : " Then had the Church rest, and grew
lazy and took things easy."

IV. SPIRITUAL UPBUILDING .. .. .. verse 31
" Edified " means more than being comforted and
instructed. "Were builded up" (R.V., margin) is its
correct meaning, a figure taken from the rise and
progress of a building.

V. HOLY LIVING .. .. verse 31
Lives lived as in the searchlight of His presence. " Walking by the fear of the Lord" (R.V., margin). Fear is
reverential awe of Him, by which we are ever conscious of His presence with us.

VI. JOY .. .. verse 31
Lives of joy in the Holy Spirit, strengthened and con-
soled by Him.

Persecutor Persecuted. The former energetic persecutor is now persecuted (verses 23-25), but his converts rescued him.

Why Saul Went to Jerusalem. He went expressly to see Peter, and spent
15 days with him (see Gal. 1. 18 to 20). Again in danger (verse 29), he
was sent to Tarsus.

Secret of Multiplication. In verse 31 we have the secret of multiplication.
Alas, most Churches these days have to report decreases. It is not enough
to shelter behind the adage, " Quality before quantity." We must have
both quality and quantity. Here is the secret of *multiplication through
quality.*

" **Then.** " " **When** ? " " Then had the Church (R.V.) rest." We do
not wonder at this, for Saul, the arch-conspirator and persecutor, had been
captured ; and the Roman Emperor, Caligula, was making an attempt to
place his own image in the Temple of Jerusalem, and sent an army to see
that it was done. The Jews therefore had enough to do to look after themselves without persecuting the Christians.

DORCAS

Dorcas was a useful woman. She was—

I. A DISCIPLE .. .. verse 36
This was an older name for the Lord's people than Christian. •

II. A SAINT .. .. verse 36
And so are all the Lord's people. But we have the experimental application of this mind. *Tabitha* is Hebrew or Syriac, and *Dorcas* Greek, for Gazelle, a graceful creature. An old-time popular name for women, suggesting beauty of form and feature, with gentleness of character and gracefulness of action. She was not only a saint, but was saintly.

III. A WORKER .. .. verses 36, 39
Not only full of good works, but also of deeds. She worked hard with her needle, excelling in practical sympathy.

IV. MISSED AND MOURNED .. .. .. verse 39
When she died she was sorely missed and greatly mourned. It is good to be missed.

From Saul to Peter. The scene suddenly shifts from Paul to Peter. This incident is introduced to show how it was that Peter was found in Joppa by the two servants of Cornelius.

An Itinerant Apostle. The persecution had scattered the Christians (chap. 8. 1). It was therefore a wise thing for Peter to visit the scattered flock.

Love Delights to Imitate. As we read these verses we are transported in thought back to the days of our Lord. Peter was moved by the Holy Spirit to speak and act as he had often heard and seen his beloved Master.

Divergence. Of course, in the very nature of things, there was a great difference. Jesus wrought miracles in His own name, whereas Peter wrought in the Name of Jesus.

Tabitha is famous as being the founder of Dorcas Societies. Though Dorcas means " gazelle," it has come to stand for companies of women formed to make garments for the poor and needy.

" While she was with them." Arresting phrase. The poor widows were able to show tangible tokens of the departed one's concern for them.

Interesting Points of Similarity. Compare Matthew 9. 7 and 25 with Acts 9.

JESUS	PETER
Put the mourners out.	" But Peter put them all forth."
" Took her by the hand."	"He gave her his hand and lifted her up."
" Arise, take up thy bed."	" Arise, and make thy bed."
" Talitha cumi " (Mark 5. 41).	" Tabitha cumi " (Acts 9. 40).

The Imitation of Jesus. If we trust, love, and serve our Lord, living and working in communion with Him, quite unconsciously we will resemble our Lord in our characters and service. " The poor bit of cloth which has held some precious piece of solid perfume will retain fragrance for many a

Continued on page 52

Continued from page 34

gave him this new name because it so well expressed the man's character, for he had unusual ability in rousing, encouraging, consoling, and strengthening.

Right View of Property. Note (1) Sale of property was quite voluntary. (2) The right of possession was not abolished. (3) The community had nothing to do with the money till it had been given them. (4) And did not share alike. (5) The distribution was according to need.

Continued from page 38

described by the apostles as fit to look after this very homely business of food and clothing : (1) Honest. (b) Not only honest men, but men *reputed* honest. (c) Full of the Holy Ghost. (d) Full of wisdom (verse 3). For such a purely secular thing as looking after a handful of poor widows, they looked for and selected men with such qualifications.

Continued from page 47

" **Saul, Saul** " (verse 4). Impressiveness is gained by the repetition.

Respectful Response. To the Voice, Saul offered a respectful response : " Sir (literally), who are Thou ? " To this inquiry we have the answer in verse 5.

Continued from page 49

" **Increased the More** " (verse 22). We do not wonder at such increase as a result of three years' waiting upon God in prayer, study of the Word, and meditation. For " confounded," M. gives " put them to confusion." " Then HIS disciples " (R.V. and 20 C.). He already had followers who had been converted to God through his ministry.

Continued from page 51

day afterwards, and will bless the scentless air by giving it forth. The man who keeps close to Christ, and has folded Him in his heart will, like the poor cloth, give forth a sweetness not his own that will gladden and refresh many nostrils."

SECTION 3

THE LORD AT WORK
EVEN UNTO
THE UTTERMOST
PARTS

ACTS 10—28

From the conversion of Saul to his martyrdom

1. **Beginning the Wider Witness, A.D. 39-44 (10—12)**
   - *(a) Peter's Vision,* the Conversion of Cornelius, and its sequel (10:1—11, 18)
   - *(b) The Church at Antioch* (11:19-20)
   - *(c) Peter's Arrest and Deliverance* (12:1-25)

2. **Paul's First Missionary Journey, A.D. 45-51 (13—14)**

   Begun at Antioch in Syria, they visited Cyprus, sailing to Perga, they mission in Antioch (in Pisida), Iconium, Lystra, Derbe, returning the same way back to Antioch.

3. **The First Great Christian Council, A.D. 51 (15:1-35)**

   The student should take special notice of the record of this council at Jerusalem, for it was of supreme importance. This gathering marked the overthrow of the first great organized attempt to mingle law with grace, Judiasm with Christianity. Thank God for the great victory.

4. Paul's Second Missionary Journey, A.D. 51-54 (15:36—18:22)

Starting again from Antioch in Syria, they missioned Tarsus, Derbe, Lystra, Iconium, Antioch. Travelling through Asia Minor they came to Troas, from whence they crossed over to Europe, landing at Neapolis and conducting services in Philippi, Thessalonica, Berea, Athens, Corinth, and Cenchrea. Sailing thence to Ephesus and on to Caesarea and Jerusalem, and ending again at Antioch. At Corinth he wrote 1 and 2 Thessalonians.

5. Paul's Third Missionary Journey, A.D. 54-58 (18:23—21:17)

Beginning once more at Antioch, they travelled to Ephesus, Philippi, Corinth, and by land to Macedonia, from whence they sailed to Tyre, calling at Troas, Assos, Miletus, and Patara, and ending at Jerusalem. At Ephesus he wrote 1 and 2 Corinthians and perhaps Hebrews, and at Corinth, Romans and Galatians.

6. Paul's Imprisonments, A.D. 58-68 (21:18-28)

(a) Imprisonment at Jerusalem (21:18—23:22)
(b) Imprisonment at Caesarea (23:23—26:32)
(c) Journey to Rome (27:1—28:15)

Continued on page 121

PREPARATION

How to get the best out of meetings

I. BEFORE A MEETING

1. **Sincerity** (2). Live up to the light you have. Cornelius had but "a farthing dip," yet he had lit it and was walking in its light.

2. **Testimony** (2). Do not keep the light to yourself. "With all his house."

3. **Prayer** (2). Live in the atmosphere of prayer. "Prayed," lit., "beseeched." No mere perfunctory prayer, not only at set times, but "always."

4. **Consistency.** Put first things first. Note how particular and scrupulous he was.

5. **Practice** (2). "Alms." Let practice follow prayer. The angel reverses in verse 4 the order in verse 2. Luke wrote as man sees, the angel as God sees.

6. **Humility** (5, 6). Though he belonged to Roman aristocracy, the great Cornelian family, a name honoured and distinguished in Roman history, he was humble enough to send for and be taught by an unknown Jew, so poor that he lodged in a tanyard.

7. **Obedience.** Military discipline pressed into religious life.

II. AT A MEETING

1. **Respect for the Messenger** (25). In the East it is usual for inferiors to prostrate themselves before men of rank and honour.

2. **Go Not Alone** (24, 27). Cornelius had his (1) *kinsmen*, (2) *near*, or intimate friends, (3) "*many*."

3. **Be All There.** Not body only, but whole heart and mind.

4. **In Worshipping Spirit.** "Before God" (33), even if meeting is only in a house.

5. **Teachable.** Be eager to hear "all things" (33), not merely the palatable, but also the unpalatable.

6. **Expectant** (33). Look for a message from God. "Command thee of God." Would to God that all preachers had messages from Him!

7. **Receive the Message.**

"**Now therefore are we all here present before God,**" etc. Thus spake Cornelius to Peter. No wonder he got such a blessing at the meeting. Why, before Peter had finished his sermon "the Holy Ghost fell on all them which heard the Word" (verse 44).

Beautiful Expression. It is a beautiful expression of entire preparedness to receive the expected teaching. The reason why so much earnest Chris-

Continued on page 121

A MODEL SERMON

Peter's utterance was a sermon that saved. Its characteristics were :

I. AN OPEN MOUTH .. .. verse 34

" Then Peter *opened his mouth*." Some preachers speak through a half-opened mouth, through their teeth. " Open thy mouth *wide* and I will fill it," is a promise that was fulfilled here.

II. A CONFESSION .. .. verses 34, 35

He prefaced his address with a confession based upon truth revealed by God. All true sermons come from God, and are based on truth revealed by Him.

III. ONE SUBJECT .. .. verse 36

The sermon was full of the Lord Jesus Christ. Note how he exalts the Saviour, and declares His universal supremacy.

IV. AN ARGUMENT .. .. verse 37

He appeals to facts they already know, and which have been abundantly substantiated.

V. A THEME .. .. verses 38-41

The Death and Resurrection of the Lord. It *touched* upon His life (38), but emphasised His death (39) and resurrection (40, 41).

VI. A WARNING .. .. verse 42

He failed not to warn, rising to lofty heights when he announces Jesus of Nazareth as Universal Judge.

VII. AN OFFER . .. . verse 43

He closes with an offer of immediate forgiveness for those who believe. At least this is as far as he got when the sermon was interrupted by the descent of the Holy Spirit.

Tangled. Peter's sermon seems a somewhat tangled utterance, " as if speech staggered under the weight of the thoughts opened up."

Object. Peter's object was to contrast the limited scope of the message, as originally confined to the children of Israel (verse 36), with its ultimate universal proclamation to all peoples and tongues.

A Parenthesis. Fancy that great statement of the universal supremacy of Jesus put down as a parenthesis ! Why, it is really the very centre of the apostle's thought. Peter points out that the Lord Jesus, who had hitherto been preached only to Israel, is really Lord of All—Jew or Gentile, and he had discovered through the vision in the Tanner's house at Joppa, that He must now be preached to all.

Use of a Parenthesis. A parenthesis is merely an interjection. True, often a qualifying interjection, yet a statement that could be left out without any injury to the sentence. In other words, a kind of superfluous

Continued on page 121

FACTS AS PROOF

An illustration of the power of Personal experience and
testimony

I. THE CENSURE .. .. verses 1-3
1. The True Report (1).
2. The Angry Contention (2). The result of prejudice.
3. The Trifling Charge (3). A mountain out of a mole hill.

II. THE REPLY .. .. verses 4-16
1. The Rehearsal of Facts (4, etc.).
2. The Claim of Divine Guidance (5, 9, 12, 15, 16). Note the
definite command of the Holy Spirit in verse 12.
3. The Irresistible Logic (17).

Peter in Hot Water. At our last meditation we left Peter in the house
of Cornelius. Whilst he was preaching, " the Holy Ghost fell on all them
which heard the Word " (10. 44). Dr. Schofield points out verse 44 as one
of the pivotal points of Scripture. Heretofore the Gospel had been offered
to Jews only, and the Holy Spirit bestowed upon believing Jews. Now the
normal order for this age is reached, for the Holy Spirit is now given without
delay, mediation, or other condition than simple faith in the Lord Jesus
Christ. After spending some days with Cornelius and his house, he returned to Jerusalem, where he got into trouble.

" **Contended.**" This is a very strong word. It was no mere discussion
or dispute. The meaning of the word is best grasped by noting its use in
Jude 9. The Devil objected to the bringing of Moses from his grave in
Moab for the Transfiguration (Matt. 17. 3), and the commands of God
could only be executed by Michael, the mighty Archangel, after a mighty
struggle with the Evil One. The Circumcision were very angry with Peter.

Peter Infallible ! Surely verse 2 proves that the early Christians did not
regard Peter as having any particular supremacy over the Church.

Absence of Prohibition. Note verse 3. Nowhere did the Lord command
them to abstain from eating with Gentiles.

Best Way to Settle Opponents is to give our own experience. A plain,
simple statement of things as they really happened. See how successful
this was as recorded in verse 18.

" **Repentance Unto Life** " (verse 18 is in 20 C. " Repentance which leads
to life ").

A NICK-NAME

The name of Christian (verse 26) was a significant nick-name, and to be worthy of this name I must be—

I. A DISCIPLE .. .. John 2. 2 ; Matt. 5. 1
> This means a scholar, and was the very first name given to the followers of the Lord Jesus Christ, and the only name used in the Gospels. It implies four things :
> 1. Coming to Christ.
> 2. Following Him.
> 3. Surrendering our wills to His.
> 4. Taught by Him.

II. ONE OF THE BRETHREN .. .. Matt. 28. 10
> Implying membership in a new family. First used by the Risen Lord. Never used by disciples until after this.

III. A NAZARENE .. .. .. Acts 2. 7 ; 24. 5
> A term of reproach implying suffering with Him.

IV. A BELIEVER .. .. Acts 5. 14
> Accepting the truths concerning His Person, Life, Death, Resurrection, etc.

V. A SAINT .. .. Acts 9. 13
> Meaning a separated one. Position not condition. Though true saints seek to make their condition (*i.e.*, holiness) like their position, *i.e.*, separation, unto God.

VI. A CHRISTIAN .. .. Acts 11. 26
> This word is only used three times in the New Testament, each with significant suggestions. See next study.

"**First at Antioch**" (verse 26). This is the statement of a patriotic individual, eager to claim all the honour he can for his native country. Luke was a native of Antioch in Syria. Here he tells us of the origin of the best name ever given to describe the followers of the Lord Jesus. And he claims the honour for his countrymen.

Another Result of the Stephen Persecution. In verses 19 to 21 we are taken back to the persecution following the death of Stephen.

Antioch was the capital of Syria, the third city in the Roman Empire. This city was more closely associated with Christianity than any other, save Jerusalem. Paul made this his base of missionary operations.

"**Preaching Jesus as Lord**," is the literal rendering, showing they proclaimed the Deity and dignity of the Saviour (verse 20). Wonderful success followed (verse 21), for they did not work alone : "Hand of the Lord was with them."

Puzzled. Thus there was founded at Antioch a large and virile Church,

Continued on page 121

CHRISTIANS

The word " Christian " occurs only three times in the Bible (Acts 11. 26 ; 26. 28 ; 1 Peter 4. 16). A Christian is :

CHILD OF GOD—Relationship   ..   ..   Gal. 3. 26
   By Birth (John 1. 12 ; 1 John 3. 1).
   By Adoption (Eph. 1. 5 ; Rom. 8. 15).

HEIR OF GOD—Prospect   ..   Rom. 8. 17 ; 1 Peter 1. 3, 4

REDEEMED—Liberty   ..   ..   Eph. 1. 7 ; Gal. 2. 13 ; 4. 5

INFLUENTIAL—Responsibility
   Salt (not Sugar) (Matt. 5. 13, 14).
   Light (Phil. 2. 15).

SOLDIER—Warfare   ..   2 Tim. 2. 3 ; Eph. 6. 10-17

TEMPLE—Indwelt   ..   1 Cor. 6. 19, 20 ; Eph. 2. 22

INSTRUMENT—Usefulness, 1 Ch. 28. 14; 2 Ch. 5. 13; Rom. 6. 13

AMBASSADOR—Representative   ..   ..   2 Cor. 5. 20
   As one sent to a foreign country (*e.g.*, Daniel in Babylon).

NEW MAN IN CHRIST—Attitude   ..   ..   2 Cor. 5. 17

" **Christian.**" This name was never used by Christians in Acts. In fact it is met with but three times, as above. It was never used by Jewish enemies, and for a very good reason—they understood its full significance.

Noble Testimony. The bestowal of this name was indeed a notable testimony to the conduct and behaviour of these early disciples. It shows they (1) Preached Christ ; (2) Lived Christ ; (3) Talked of Christ ; (4) Worshipped Christ ; (5) Glorified Christ ; (6) Prayed to Christ ; (7) Resembled Christ in some particulars.

Jesuists. Is it not remarkable that they did not call them Jesuists ? They gave them their name not from the name of His person, Jesus ; but of His office, Christ. To be called Jesuists would have meant they were followers of a mere man.

Glory. The name given in contempt we glory in. By degrees it was adopted by the disciples and worn as an honour.

Are we Worthy to Bear It ? Alexander the Great was perturbed to find a soldier in his army bearing his name who was a coward. " Either change thy name or mend thy manners," said he to that individual.

A Christian is :
   (1) *A Disciple* (Acts 11. 26).
   (2) *A Soul-Winner* (Acts 26. 28). Agrippa said in effect : " Paul, you are doing your best to persuade me to be a Christian."
   (3) *A Sufferer* (1 Peter 4. 16) for Christ and His cause.
      (*a*) Not being ashamed of Him.
      (*b*) Glorying in the suffering when it is to His glory.

A GOOD MAN

Barnabas is described as "a good man" (24), and illustrates some of the elements that go to make up goodness

I. BELIEVING   ..   ..   ..   Acts 4. 32, 36, 37

Faith in the Saviour made a wonderful change in this Levite. Probably one of the converts at Pentecost. He became a man of prayer, and a student of one Book, the Scriptures.

II. BRAVE   ..   ..   Acts 9. 26, 27

An espouser of an unpopular cause.

III. SEPARATED   ..   ..   ..   Acts 13. 2, 4

For a specific mission and duty.

IV. FULL OF FAITH ..   ..   Acts 11. 24

Faith is the foundation of Christian character and service.

V. FULL OF THE HOLY SPIRIT ..   ..   Acts 11. 24

This was the fountain with an everlasting spring.

VI. GOOD   ..   ..   Acts 11. 24

Not mere human goodness, but that which came from God.

VII. GENEROUS   ..   ..   Acts 4. 37

He possessed a farm, but sold it, and then had to support himself by manual toil.

VIII. SYMPATHETIC   ..   ..   ..   Acts 4. 36 ; 9. 27

Given by the apostles a new name, " Barnabas," meaning " *The Consoler*," as expressing so well the man's character.

IX. UNSELFISH   ..   ..   Acts 11. 23

Rejoicing in success granted to others, and work done by others.

X. SUCCESSFUL   ..   ..   Acts 11. 24

" Much people added unto the Lord," the truest success.

XI. SELF-EFFACING ..   ..   Acts 13. 2, 46

The story of the missionary journey begins with Barnabas and Saul, but very soon Paul and Barnabas. Though Barnabas was older in years and grace, he did not resent taking second place. To " play second fiddle " when he had been so long a leader was a great test of character.

XII. HUMAN   ..   ..   Acts 15. 39

Though a great man of God, he was truly human. Here Barnabas yielded to family affection and manifested a strange stubbornness. But he continued to work for the Lord. Paul referred to him very tenderly and lovingly twenty-seven years afterwards.

PRAYER

The Prayer that brought deliverance was :

I. INSTANT

A.V., *margin*. No delay. To postpone means often to kill all true prayer. Pray when the mood comes as well as at stated times.

II. EARNEST

R.V., *margin*. No cold, formal, lifeless prayer, but prayer offered with fervour.

III. PERSISTENT

"*Without ceasing.*" No mere formal presentation of petitions and then leaving it. It was clamorous.

A week of prayer. From "days of unleavened bread" till "after Easter."

IV. UNITED

"Of the Church." Union is strength.

V. ENCOURAGED

By past deliverance (Acts 5. 19). A while before, all the apostles were imprisoned, but God delivered them. Might He not now deliver Peter ?

VI. SUBMISSIVE AND CHASTENED

The death of James would show them that God did not always mean to interpose. Perhaps the execution of James was so hurried that the Church did not know of it until afterwards.

VII. TESTED

The answer was not given until the last moment, when hope was almost dead.

VIII. ANSWERED   See next Study.

"**But**" (verse 5). What an eloquent "But" this is ! There is a vital connection between prayer and Peter's escape. There is another eloquent "But" in this chapter (see 24).

Last Time Peter Mentioned. This chapter is notable because, after this, Peter is dropped out of the history of the Acts, and is scarcely heard of again. There is just one more glimpse of him in Acts 15, when he championed Paul who had got into trouble with the Judaizers, as he had done. But with that exception, here is the last mention of him in the Acts.

New Persecution. Here is noticed a new persecution and persecutor. The Herod here was grandson of the Herod who sought the life of the infant Saviour. What a strange Defender of the Faith to be sure !

"**He Killed James**" (verse 2). Here is recorded the death of one of the inner circle (Peter, James, and John) of disciples. James is the ONLY apostle whose death is recorded in Scripture. Is not this a remarkable omission ! A beautiful incident connected with his martyrdom is related by Clement of Alexandria, and preserved in Eusebius' Ecclesiastical

Continued on page 122

DELIVERANCE

Peter's deliverance from prison is an emblem of a greater deliverance, that from the power of sin.

I. THE BONDAGE
    1. By an Outside Power.
    2. Secure and Hopeless. Soldiers, 4 ; Two Chains, Keepers, 6 ; Iron Gate, Two Wards, 10.
    3. The Enslaved One Asleep.

II. THE DELIVERANCE
    1. Approach of the Lord's Messenger.
    2. Light. (Light before the deliverance reveals the bondage more clearly).
    3. Awakened by a Touch.
    4. On Obedience, Chains are Snapped.
    5. Clothing and Preparation for a Journey.
    6. Guidance by God's Messenger.

Private and Public. Evidently James' execution had taken place privately and hurriedly. Herod purposed to butcher Peter publicly seven days later to make a Jewish holiday. It was a crowded time in Jerusalem, and the spectacle of an apostle's execution was to be their sport and pastime in the interval of religious duty.

Delay. The Feast of Unleavened Bread caused a seven days' delay, but Herod, determined to make Peter's escape impossible, put him in a secure prison guarded by sixteen soldiers.

Prayer Answered in an Unexpected Fashion, at the last moment when hope was almost dead. The whole story is varied and full of detail :
    (a) Peter slept. Third time he is found sleeping. 1st, Mount of Transfiguration. 2nd, Garden of Gethsemane. Here it was a notable triumph of faith. The calm sleep of the condemned man tells of a trustful and submissive heart.
    (b) Angel's solicitude for Peter's comfort (verse 8). Angel would not do for Peter what he could do for himself (verses 8. 11).
    (c) When he was left to himself he comes to himself (verse 10. 11).
    (d) Rhoda, the slave girl, through joy forgetting plain and pressing duties (verse 14).
    (e) Peter did not enter when the door was opened (verse 17).
    (f) Prayer place not disclosed, for evidently it was still being used, and the host might get into trouble.

A Gospel Application. Peter's deliverance can be taken as an emblem of a greater deliverance, that from moral bondage, with an application to the unsaved sinner, and to the uninstructed and not fully delivered believer.

Two Touches. In this chapter we have two recorded touches of the angel, with two directly opposite results (verses 7 and 23). Here is a solemn reminder. Resist not the first touch, else it may have the opposite effect to that desired.

Prosperity of the Church. Note the progress in spite of the persecution 2. 41 ; 4. 32 ; 5. 14 ; 6. 7 ; 8. 25 ; 9. 31 ; 11. 24, etc.

MINISTERING

Ministering to the Lord means :

I. WORSHIP

Silent and audible praise. Adoration. Oh, the blessedness of such holy exercise.

II. WAITING

Spending as much time in silence before the Lord as already spent in presenting petitions.

III. HEARKENING

The fat of rams was a portion specially sacred and set apart only for the Lord. Yet " hearkening " is of greater value (1 Sam. 15. 22). When they listened, God spake.

IV. PRAYING

They fasted and prayed in order to ascertain, then secure grace to do the will of God.

V. WORKING

What a joy it is to render our service in a worshipping mood.

New Era. In chapter 13 a new Church era dawns. Remember the command of the Saviour (Acts 1. 8). By this time the Gospel had been preached in (a) Jerusalem, then (b) Judea and Samaria, now (c) the last phase is about to be inaugurated—" The uttermost parts of the earth." Now Jerusalem ceases to be the centre, Antioch, and later Rome, taking its place. Jerusalem had ceased to be the centre because it had failed to discern and yield to the Divine indications of widening purposes.

Some Outstanding Personalities. In verse 1 we find reference to several believers of outstanding ability. Barnabas, the converted Levite ; Simeon Niger, *i.e.*, Simeon the Black. He was called Black because of his dark complexion by birth, or long residence in a tropical country. Probably he was an African. Some suppose he was the same one who bore our Lord's Cross (Matt. 27. 32). Lucius of Cyrene, North Africa, is mentioned in Romans 16. 21. Manaen was foster-brother to the Herod who was the one in power when our Lord began His work. Rich and poor, educated and illiterate, were amongst the followers of Christ. Saul, last mentioned, but not the least.

Special Burden. Evidently some special burden was pressing on their hearts and minds. Undoubtedly that burden was concerning the heathen around them. This Church had been looking after the bodies of the people (11. 27 to 30), now they were exercised about the starving souls around them. Have we ever been so exercised about the state of the unconverted that we have lost our appetite for food, or voluntarily fasted and given ourselves to prayer ?

Sent Forth by the Church (verse 3), yet by the Holy Ghost (verse 4).

Unselfishness. Saul and Barnabas were their ministers. Many owed their conversion under God to them. Yet they promptly obeyed the Divine voice. What unselfishness !

AN APOSTATE

This Sorcerer at Paphos was :

I. A JEW .. .. verses 8, 10

One who had enjoyed the light, but had evidently deliberately thrown it over, hence an apostate.

II. A PROFANE JEW .. .. verse 10

His very name was a profanation. *Bar*, Syriac for Son, " Son of Jesus." Yet he was a " son of the Devil."

III. A CLEVER JEW .. .. verse 8

Elymas is Arabic for " The Wise " or " Magi," the same name for the Wise Men of the East who went to worship the infant Saviour.

IV. A BLIND JEW .. .. verse 11

The blindness was typical of his true state. The closing of his eyes led to the opening of the eyes of the Roman official.

Paphos. A journey of about 100 miles from Antioch. Paphos was the seat of the vile worship of Venus, indeed was supposed to have been her birthplace.

Sergius Paulus. The willingness and eagerness of the educated Romans for light and truth in the New Testament is noticeable. The fact being that the average Roman was conscious of the hollowness of their heathen faith, and longed for light.

False Teachers. How indignant we are to notice that those who knew better took advantage of their eagerness to palm off their acquired superstition.

Paul's Scathing Rebuke. What a scathing rebuke we have in verses 9 to 11. The Holy Spirit does not always move His servants to speak in honeyed terms.

Two Notable Sayings. " Desired to hear the Word of God " (verse 7). " Doctrine of the Lord " (verse 12).

A CHANGE OF NAME

This was a significant change of name from Saul (Hebrew)
to Paul (Roman).

I. REASON

The Fruit of a Changed Life. In heathen lands to-day
Christian converts select new names. So after his
conversion Saul became Paul.

II. SIGNIFICANCE

An Indication of a Deepening Spiritual Life. Saul means
desired, Paul means *little*. He was small in stature
and also in his own estimation. One sign of growth
in grace is a growing depreciation of oneself, and a
growing appreciation of the Lord Jesus Christ. As
John the Baptist said : " He must increase but I
must decrease."

III. MEMORIAL

A Memorial of a Great Victory. Paul (verse 7) was the
name of Saul's first notable convert. Great con-
querors have been named after great victories.
Paul's new name was a standing memorial to this
great victory. Christianity (Paul) condemned sor-
cery (Bar-jesus) and converted rationalism (Sergius
Paulus).

IV. RECOGNITION

A Recognition of his Life's Work. Saul is Hebrew,
Paul is Roman. Recognising his call to Gentile
ministry, he strips himself of his Jewish name. The
only way to help people is to reach down to their
level.

Change. From this time two changes are to be noticed. There is a
change in the order of the names. Saul is last in verse 1, last also in verse
2, but leader in verse 13 and onward. Then, secondly, not only in the
order of the names, but in the names themselves.

Why ? We know why criminals change their names ; why Jews sometimes for trade purposes change their names ; why heirs change their
names in accordance with the wishes of their benefactor ; but why did
Saul change his name to Paul ? See above outline.

New Name. " Write Thy new name upon my heart,
         Thy new best name of Love ! "

FORGIVENESS OF SINS

The forgiveness of sins is an experience which is—

I. REAL
A solid and substantial thing. Nothing imaginary about it. It rests on the Death and Resurrection of the Lord Jesus Christ, and upon His word.

II. ELEMENTARY
It is of first necessity to the sinner, the first experienced blessing of the Gospel.

III. VITAL
Without it a man is not a Christian at all. It is fundamental to all other spiritual blessings, the very basis of Christian experience.

IV. COMPLETE
It means more than being let off. It means " cutting-off," excision. Forgiveness is a complete gift.

V. FRUITFUL
Because of what follows, justification, peace, etc.

VI. REPEATED
We need daily forgiveness, as our Lord taught in the Lord's Prayer.

Paul's First Recorded Utterance. Here we have the first recorded public utterance of Paul since his conversion. Not, of course, his maiden speech, but the first recorded speech. It is worthy of note that in the first recorded utterance we have a brief statement of the doctrine of Justification by Faith.

Antioch. This sermon was delivered in Antioch in Pisidia, 100 miles from the other Antioch (13. 1).

" Sat Down." Those acquainted with ancient Synagogue customs, state that the phrase " Sat down," is significant, implying that they were not listeners only, but teachers. They sat, as it were, in the seat of the Rabbis, and their doing so was an indication that they asked for permission to address the congregation.

Time of Year. Paul quotes from Deuteronomy 1. 31 and Isaiah 1. 1 to 27, and these were the Synagogue lessons for the 44th Sabbath in the year, our July or August.

Modelled after Stephen. This speech follows very closely Stephen's dying utterance. He and Paul began with the history of God's covenant with the Jewish nation, and ended by preaching Jesus and the Resurrection, finally giving a solemn warning.

Culminating Point. Verse 38 is the point Paul had been working up to.

A Great Forgiveness. A poor criminal in Scotland, as he went forth to the place of execution, kept crying out : " He is a great Forgiver ! He is a great Forgiver ! "

ETERNAL LIFE

The Qualifications for Eternal Life

I. SELF-KNOWLEDGE

To know oneself to be unworthy. To judge oneself worthy for eternal life is proof that one is unworthy and unfitted for no one is worthy.

II. NOT OF WORKS

To abandon all effort to make oneself worthy. It is " Just as I am, without one plea, but that Thy Blood was shed for me."

III. EARNEST DESIRE

To really desire Eternal Life. Some of God's gifts He bestows unconditionally, but He never gives His choicest gifts until there is real and heart-felt desire, leading to a right valuation of the gift.

IV. SIMPLE ACCEPTANCE

To accept Eternal Life on God's terms, *i.e.*, as a gift. The result,—" filled with joy " (52), though they had just been won from heathendom, and their guides, Paul and Barnabas, had been hunted out of Antioch.

Unmannerly. Such a sermon had never been preached in the Synagogue at Antioch in Pisidia. Results were immediate. Some Jews were unmannerly enough to leave before the meeting was over (verse 42). The Gentile proselytes who remained, begged to hear the message again next Sabbath. Some of his hearers followed Paul out.

A Miserable Motive. Next Sabbath the Synagogue was packed out " to hear the Lord's message " (W.). " Waxed bold " is in W. " Throwing off all reserve." The unconverted Jews were angry at such popularity. What a miserable motive for antagonism !

An Important Decision. This opposition clarified thought, and Paul and Barnabas put into plain words the law of their future conduct (verse 46). There is a touch of righteous indignation about Paul's outburst.

" **Judge** " (verse 46). Authorities state that the word " Judge " here has not the loose sense usually understood in ordinary conversation. It does not mean " estimate," " consider," " think." It must be taken in its judicial sense. They were their own judges, not Paul or Barnabas. By their own act they sentenced themselves. In rejecting the Gospel they passed sentence upon themselves.

" **Judge yourselves unworthy of everlasting life** " (verse 46). That was the farthest thought from their minds. What an unusual expression. What a fertile brain Paul had. His vocabulary was rich and pregnant. It is an expression that attracts and grips. Contrast it with verse 48.

" **Ordained.** " The word here has the meaning of " fitted." " All those believed who were ready for enduring life " (20 C.).

THE BIBLE

Some of the inspired names for the Bible given us :

I. ITS SOURCE .. .. Psa. 107. 11 ; 1 Thess. 2. 13
"**The Words of God,**" to be received.

II. ITS AUTHORITY .. .. .. Eccles. 8. 4
"**The Word of a King,**" to be upheld.

III. ITS CHARACTER .. .. .. Job 6. 10
"**The Words of the Holy One,**" to be revealed.

IV. ITS INSPIRATION .. .. Job 23. 12 ; Isa. 55. 11
"**The Words of His Mouth,**" to be esteemed.

V. ITS FINALITY. .. .. 2 Tim. 2. 15 ; Eph. 1. 13
"**The Word of Truth,**" to be studied.

VI. ITS RELIABILITY .. .. .. Titus 1. 9
"**The Faithful Word,**" to be held fast.

VII. ITS MESSAGE, to be delivered
1. "**The Word of Thy Righteousness** (Psa. 119. 123).
2. "**The Word of Promise** " (Rom. 9. 9).
3. "**The Word of His Grace** " (Acts 14. 3 ; 20. 32).
4. "**The Word of Reconciliation** " (2 Cor. 5. 19).
5. "**The Word of Life** " (Phil. 2. 16).
6. "**The Word of My Patience** (Rev. 3. 10).

From Antioch to Iconium (13. 51) was a long journey, over wild, dangerous mountains.

New Method of opposition. Here the unbelieving Jews adopted a new method of attack. They moved the Gentiles (verse 2), not against the apostles, but sought to blacken the character of the new converts (lovely name—Brethren !). These new converts bore the brunt of the persecution. It was a cunning move. But Paul stayed a " long time " (verse 3) on that very account. He would not leave his friends if he could help it.

" **Word of His Grace** " (verse 3). What a delightful name for the Bible ! When your copy of His Word requires rebinding, and you can select the name, have you ever thought that you can make a selection from twelve inspiring titles? My favourite is " The Word of His Patience." Here " The Word of His Grace " signifying, 1st, Its Origin (the Grace of God). 2nd, Gift (pure act of God's Grace). 3rd, Message (the unmerited favour of God). Study the above list of inspired names.

GOD'S WITNESSES

Are varied and wonderfully convincing in their separate and united testimony.   Here are some :

I. PROVIDENCE .. .. verse 17
1. God is not inactive.   " *He did* good."
2. He is not a revengeful Deity.   " He did *good.*"   He does good because He is good.
3. He is not a Gloomy Being.   " Filling our hearts with... *gladness.*"

II. NATURE .. .. verses 15, 17
1. Orderly sequence of seasons.
2. Yearly miracle of harvest.
3. Variety in Creation—hills, mountains, sea.

III. CONSCIENCE
An invisible witness, securely entrenched within the city of mansoul.

IV. THE BIBLE
The Bible is a wonderful Witness for God.

V. THE LORD JESUS CHRIST, ... Heb. 1. 2
Who is the greatest Witness of all ?   God's " Last Word."

VI. CHRISTIANS .. .. Eph. 2. 7
Are God's witnesses on earth, and will be His witnesses in eternity.

A Keep-Sake. " Keep-sakes " are often given by friends about to die or emigrate.   It is pathetic to note man's desire to live in the memories of others.   Here in verse 17, Paul declares that God has given many keep-sakes.   This he did both before and after man had fallen.   Ah, even in the " Far Country " we cannot get away from His witnesses.

Lystra was an important military centre in Paul's day.   Apparently it was without a Synagogue, though there were a few Jews, such as Timothy and his mother and grandmother.

A Significant Omission. Have you noted the remarkable omission of the Saviour's Name in Paul's command to the cripple ?   Was this the reason why the attention of the people was drawn to Paul and Barnabas, and not to his Lord, and so much so that they purposed worshipping them ?

Heaven Not Indifferent !   The action of the people of Lystra shows how deep in the human heart lies the belief that, if there be a God, He cannot leave earth's miseries unpitied and unhelped.

An Objection. In verse 16 Paul meets an objection which rises in his mind as likely to be in his hearers', viz., if there is such a God, why have we not heard of Him till now ?   So Paul points out that God had not left them without witnesses to Him.

THREE DOORS

I. DOOR OF FAITH .. .. verse 27

Not of works. The door of entrance into the fold of Christ is that of faith.

II. DOOR OF OPPORTUNITY 1 Cor. 16. 9; 2 Cor. 2. 12; Rev.3.8

A suitable outlet of service for ardent spirits aflame with the love of God.

III. DOOR OF UTTERANCE .. .. .. Col. 4. 3

The wonderful liberty, both in spirit and of speech, communicated by the Spirit of God to the consecrated and dependent servant of the Lord.

Malice of Jews. Paul's bitter Jewish opponents travelled all the way from Antioch and Iconium to oppose the truth (verse 19), and the result being that the people who one day were prepared to worship God's servants, now kill Paul. Oh, the folly of building on the applause of men ! What a fleeting thing it is to be sure !

" **Drew Him Out**." An added touch of brutality. Not satisfied by killing him (for no one could be stoned and live), they dragged the corpse out of the city with no gentle hands, adding insult to injury. Without doubt, the experience Paul relates in 2 Corinthians 12. 1 to 4, took place at this very moment. Paul wrote 2 Corinthians 14 years after he was stoned at Lystra.

" **The Disciples** " (verse 20). Then God had given them converts here !

" **Returned again to Lystra** " (verse 21). What courage ! " Confirming," *i.e.*, establishing.

Measures Taken for the Continuance of the Work are shown in verse 23. " When they had ordained them elders."

THE COUNCIL

The First Great Council of the Christian Church and its
Momentous Decision

I. PUBLIC RECEPTION .. .. verse 4
At which the Judaizers made their protest
(verse 5).

II. PRIVATE CONVERSATIONS .. .. Gal. 2. 1, 2
Between Paul and Barnabas and James,
Peter, and John.

III. GREAT CONFERENCE
1 First Address given by Peter (verses 7-11).
2. Second Address given by Barnabas and Paul
(verse 12).
3. Third Address given by James, the brother
of our Lord (verse 13-21).
4. The First Christian Letter containing the
great Charter of Gentile Christian Liberty
(verses 22-29).

Fourteen Years had passed since Paul's conversion and strenuous Gospel
compaigns. The revival tide had arisen until it had overflowed the strict
Jewish barriers, and had broken down the partition walls, to the con-
sternation of many of the Pharisees, who, after the example of Paul, had
been converted to Christ; but unlike him, had not surrendered Jewish
bigotry and legal ceremonial (see 15. 1).

A Deputation. At last the Church at Antioch determined to send a
deputation to Jerusalem in order to settle these vexed and vexing points
(verse 2), as they had not (what we now possess) a New Testament as the
final rule of faith and conduct. They were brought on their way by the
Church (verse 3). Their progress was more like a triumphal procession.

Interesting Points. (1) Characteristically in Jerusalem, Barnabas is
temporarily restored to his place above Paul. He speaks first, and was
regarded by the Church as the superior. (2) James calls Peter by an
intensely Jewish name—Simeon, the name Peter calls himself in his
Second Epistle. (3) " Subverting your souls " (verse 24) is in W., " Un-
settled your minds." (4) " *Beloved* Barnabas and Paul " (verse 25), thus
rebuking the attacks of the Judaizers upon them. (C) " Confirmed " in
verse 32 is in W. " strengthened."

JOHN MARK

A Warning to the Impulsive and an Encouragement to the
Defeated

I. IN THE GARDEN OF GETHSEMANE   Mark 14. 51, 52
Why we think this unnamed young man was Mark :
1. It is a trivial incident, of no interest to any but Mark.
2. The minuteness of the story suggests personal history.
3. The conduct is in harmony with character of Mark,
   a man of fine impulses and generous enthusiasm, but
   lacking in steadfast and resolute courage.
4. The garment mentioned was only worn by the wealthy.
   Mark was the son of a well-to-do Christian woman.
5. This may explain the records of details of the Lord's
   prayers in Gethsemane when all the disciples were
   asleep. Mark was a hidden watcher.

II. ASSISTING PAUL AND BARNABAS   Acts 12. 25

III. THE FAINT-HEARTED ONE .. .. Acts 13. 13
In Asia Minor the three missionaries were about to cross
the Taurus Mountains and strike inland. These were
rough and toilsome, with a bad reputation for brigands
and outlaws. This was too much for Mark, who
deserted his companions and returned to his home
and mother, ease and comfort. This was not a
departure from the Lord, but from duty.

IV. THE CAUSE OF DISSENSION ..   Acts 15. 37-41
1. Two painful scenes at Antioch before Paul left for his
   second missionary journey, first, the rebuking of Peter
   and Barnabas (Gal. 2. 11-15), then, quarrel with
   Barnabas.
2. The second journey was to take them back to the very
   region Mark jibbed at.
3. Was Paul right ?   Evidently Church at Antioch
   thought so, for they recommended Paul and Silas to
   the Grace of God (40), but no record of doing so to
   Barnabas and Mark.
4. But good came out of evil, two missionary parties
   started instead of one.

V. THE RECLAIMED ONE Col. 4. 10, 12; Phile. 24; 2 Tim.4.11
1. Twenty years later Paul refers to Mark in glowing
   terms.
2. How is this ? By the grace of God he had developed
   into a brave and faithful soldier of the Lord Jesus.
   The one whom Paul once discarded as useless and

Continued on page 122

PAUL'S COMPANION

Significant acts associated with the setting apart of a New
Gospel companion for the Apostle Paul

I. GRACE

Timothy was converted during Paul's first visit seven
years before (1 Tim. 1. 2). It is supposed that the
sight of Paul's sufferings led this tenderly nurtured
youth to a definite decision for Christ. Wondrous
grace !

II. ACCREDITED

Must have been quite a youth, for twelve years afterwards Paul calls him a youth (1 Tim. 4. 12). Why
take such a young and untrained youth when he had
refused Mark ? Because of the good opinion of
fellow-believers.

III. PRUDENCE

Paul took Silas with him on this new missionary
journey. Seeing another name was in the apostolic
letter Paul carried about with him, it was an act of
prudence as well as of wisdom to employ Timothy
also.

IV. EXPEDIENCY

Why circumcise him ? Was this inconsistent ? It was
both an act of prudence and of expediency, in order
to placate the bigoted Jews of that part. Note, he
was already a saved man.

V. ORDINATION

After circumcision, Paul ordained Timothy, the
order being :

1. Preaching (1 Tim. 1. 18).
2. Searching examination of character and profession
   of faith (1 Tim. 6. 12).
3. Laying on of hands (1 Tim. 4. 14).

" **Came to Derbe and Lystra** " (verse 1). Nothing is told of the journey
from Antioch, though much no doubt had befallen them *en route*. Seven
years had passed since Paul's first visit recorded in Acts 14, yet the work of
God begun then had prospered.

Timothy. This is the first time Timothy's name is mentioned.

Established (verse 5). It is one thing to be " in the faith," and another
to be established. " Established 50 years," we sometimes see outside
business houses or on their printed announcements. But they are mistaken.
The business was *started* 50 years ago, but for years was a poor struggling
cause ; inaugurated 50 years ; *established* 20 years ! Many Christians never
seem to get *established*. Let God have His own way with you then you will
be established as a tree planted by rivers of water (see Psalm 1).

A GUIDED MAN

Two Studies on Guidance : 1st, The Man who was Guided.
Paul had already been guided in four ways, *i.e.*, into :

I. THE TRUTH OF GOD ..   ..   ..   John 16. 13
     1. Concerning Himself.
     2. Concerning the Saviour.
     3. Concerning the Christian Faith.
     4. Concerning Christian People.

II. THE FAMILY OF GOD ..   ..   John 1. 12 ; 3. 5
     No entrance into the family of God save by the New
     Birth by the Holy Spirit.

III. THE LIBERTY OF GOD   ..   Isa. 10. 2 ; Rom. 8. 2
     1. From the Guilt of Sin.
     2. From the Bondage of Sin.
     3. From the Bondage of Ritualism.

IV. ENTIRE DEVOTION TO GOD ..   ..   Rom. 12. 1, 2
     To discover the acceptable and perfect will of God,
     consecration is essential.

" **Assuredly gathering that the Lord had called us** " (Acts 16. 10). And
we know they were not mistaken. Humanly speaking, the entrance of the
Gospel into Europe depended upon that decision. If they had not paid
attention to all the indications of the Divine will, and had followed the
course they themselves had mapped out, Europe would have been left
in the dark.

Puzzle. Divine guidance is a puzzle to many. Oh, the pity of it ! The
very thing that was intended for our comfort to puzzle, bewilder, and
distress us !

Repelled. True to say we have often been repelled by certain claims to
Divine guidance. The mistake many make is they do not test their
impulses. A strong impulse may be a temptation from the Devil.

Not Abnormal. Divine guidance, instead of being an abnormal experience, should really be the normal experience of every child of God
(Rom. 8. 14).

The Man who was Led. This is an important point. The majority of
those puzzled over this subject are in a faulty spiritual condition.

METHODS OF GUIDANCE

A Second Study on Divine Guidance

I. GODLY DESIRE .. ..   Acts 15. 36

Given by the Spirit. Whilst no doubt praying, he was possessed of a desire to re-visit the Churches planted during the first tour.

II. INWARD RESTRAINT .. .. verse 6

We are not told how they discovered the restraint of the Spirit. Was it through a prophetic message? Or was it an inward conviction through the secret whispers in the mind by the Spirit.

III. OUTWARD HINDRANCE .. .. .. verse 7

Providence blocked the way. Be ready and willing to be taught by and through failures and hindrances.

IV. VISION FROM CHRIST .. .. verse 9

The form of the vision is striking—not a command from Christ, but a petition from man.

V. CONSULTATION .. .. verse 10

At verse 10 begins the " we " of the Acts, from which we conclude that Luke now joined them. It also suggests serious consultation. " Assuredly gathering " is a picturesque sentence. It literally means " laying things together." We must not act on untested impulses. Time is not wasted in making sure of the meaning of special providences.

Why our Attention is Specially Drawn to this incident. The book of the Acts is careful to point out how each fresh step in the extension of the work was taken.

Natural. One is struck by the perfect naturalness of the whole story. Paul meant a short tour, just going over old Gospel battlefields, but Christ meant—Europe!

Step by Step. Observe, guidance came step by step.

OPENED

Some of the Opened Things in the Word of God

I. BOOK FOR INSTRUCTION .. .. Neh. 8. 4, 5

This is the first time that pulpit is mentioned in the Word. Big enough to hold thirteen men. After opening the Book they read on for several hours. Note verse 8. Probably during the exile the greater part of the Jews had forgotten their mother tongue. Thus it was necessary to explain the Hebrew.

II. EAR FOR LISTENING .. .. .. Isa. 50. 4, 5

Literally " the tongue of the learner." The tongue is influenced by the ear.

III. EYES FOR SEEING .. .. .. Acts 9. 8

Blinded literally for a season.

IV. MIND FOR UNDERSTANDING .. .. Luke 24. 45

That is, for understanding the Scriptures.

V. HEART FOR CONVERSION .. .. Acts 16. 14

Opened hearts receive first the written Word and then Christ the Living Word.

VI. DOOR FOR ADMISSION .. .. Acts 14. 27

The door of faith into the fold of God.

VII. WINDOW FOR BLESSING .. .. Mal. 3. 10

Not pray but prove. To pray is always well. But to pray while we are withholding from God is useless.

VIII. MOUTH FOR TESTIMONY .. .. Eph. 6. 19

Speakers know what liberty of spirit and liberty of utterance mean.

" **Certain Days** " (verse 12) they were in the city, then they heard of a few women who met at stated times for prayer by a river side (verse 13), when Paul and his companions joined them. The mightiest thing done in Europe that morning was this act of Paul.

Insignificant. Yet how insignificant it seems. Just a few women gathered for prayer ! Much Christian work is apparently insignificant yet great. What is done for and in God is always great.

Fortune-telling. " As we went to prayer " (verse 16). Were they on their way to the river-side oratory ? Fortune-telling is of the Devil.

"**Many days**" (verse 18). This was more than God's servants could allow.

" **When her Masters,**" etc. (verse 19). The root of the first antagonism to the Gospel in Europe was purely mercenary.

" **The Lord Opened** " (verse 14). Divine co-operation. How busy the Lord is ! Note the steps in her conversion : (1) *Attention.* She " heard." (2) *Conviction.* " She attended." (3) *Conversion.* " Heart the Lord opened." (4) *Obedience.* " She was baptised." (5) *Generosity.* " Come into my house."

Three Conversions are here recorded, representing different walks in life : (1) *A Woman,* for commerce or business. (2) *A Girl,* for service. (3) *A Man,* a jailer for government. And the Gospel appeals to each and conquers each.

TWO CONVERSIONS

A Study in Contrast. Lydia and the Jailer.

I. A WOMAN—A MAN
Both of whom found full satisfaction in the same Saviour.

II. A MERCHANT—A JAILER
Though forbidden to preach in Asia, Paul's first convert in Europe was an Asiatic—Lydia. God's ways are wonderful.

III. REFINED—VULGAR
An educated lady and a coarse, rough soldier.

IV. INDUSTRIOUS—CARELESS
The jailer slept at his post (27) dressed, his sword beside him.

V. PIOUS—IRRELIGIOUS
She worshipped God (14). Believed in prayer and practised it. He was superstitious and irreligious.

VI. TENDER—CRUEL
She offered hospitality. He improved or added to his instructions (24).

VII. CONVERTED IN QUIET—IN NOISE
One was gradual and the other sudden.

VIII. REVERENCE—FEAR AND AWE
Paul's words freed the jailer from all fear (27, 28), only to awaken to a less selfish and profounder awe (29).

IX. NO QUESTION—A QUESTION
She opened gently like a bud to the sun. He was rock that earthquake had to rend.

X. SOUGHT FOR—SEEKING (29)
Why did he act thus ? Had he the girl's message ? (17).

XI. BEFORE HOSPITALITY—AFTER HOSPITALITY

XII. DAY TIME—MIDNIGHT

XIII. INTELLIGENT—IGNORANT
The jailer knew very little of the Lord Jesus. How many who know far more never ask the same question ? Paul's answer is blessedly short and clear. See how little it takes to secure salvation.

Contrast. Two real and definite conversions to God are recorded in this chapter. But what a contrast between the two ! God has not made two of us alike, neither are we saved in precisely the same manner.

"**They Comforted Them**" (verse 40). Remarkable statement. One

Continued on page 122

PRISON SONGS

Like birds singing in a darkened cage. A Study of the Song
of the Lord, " THE NEW SONG "

I. BEGINS ON THE ROCK .. .. Psa. 40. 3
  Salvation possible only by a Power outside of ourselves.

II. CONTINUES IN THE ROCK .. .. Isa. 42. 11
  In troublous times Eastern folk left their homes in the
  plains and valleys, and dwelt in rocky heights.

III. ENRICHED BY CONSECRATION .. 2 Chron. 29. 27
  " How can we sing the Lord's song in a strange land ? "
  (Psa. 137. 4). When we offer ourselves as living sacri-
  fices to God in an act of consecration.

IV. INCREASES WITH KNOWLEDGE .. Isa. 24. 14
  As our knowledge of the Lord increases, so shall the
  volume of praise.

V. HELPED BY PRAYER .. .. .. Acts 16. 25
  The song had been beaten out of them. As they lay
  with bleeding backs on the filthy dungeon floor, they
  began to pray, then the Lord gave songs in the night.

Darkened Cage. One has quaintly remarked : " These birds could sing
in a darkened cage."

A Parable. It is a puzzle how gloom and sadness has become associated
in so many minds with our Christian faith. The Bible is a Book of singing.
Even in the most solemn of all the Bible books, the Book of Revelation,
there is a great gladness and joy. If " woe " is mentioned nine times,
there are ten songs sung by eight different choirs (4. 8 to 11 ; 5. 8 to 14 ;
7. 9 to 12).

Redemption. It is a remarkable fact that the only singing in the Bible
is connected with Redemption. Even angels are never said to " sing."
" Praising God and *saying* " (not singing) (Luke 2. 13). " They sang a new
song...and no man could learn that song save...they that were redeemed "
(Rev. 5. 9 ; 14. 3). The lesson is obvious—there can be no true joy and
happiness apart from God and His wonderful salvation.

ENCOURAGEMENT

Why Paul the Despondent became Paul the Energetic Enthusiast. It was the result of :

I. THE WORD OF GOD

The Constraining Power of the Word within him, compelling him to give utterance to it. Some portion of God's Word had appealed specially to him. He was now in the grip of the Word. It augurs ill for a man's grip of the Word if that Word does not grip him.

II. A MESSAGE FROM THE LORD

An encouraging message from the Master Himself. See what the Lord did for His much-tried servant (9, 10). How timely !

III. THOUGHTS OF OTHERS .. 2 Cor. 1. 8 ; 4. 8

Note the " we." The trials that have come to us are but common to all.

IV. PAST LABOURS

Discovery that past labours were not in vain. His two companions brought good news from Thessalonica, scattering his gloomy forebodings. This encouraged him to new activity.

V. FINANCIAL RELIEF .. .. Phil 4. 15 ; 2 Cor. 11.9

He was relieved from the necessity of tent-making by the money contributed by the Philippians, enabling him to labour in the Gospel more freely.

What Despondent Ones Should Do. Keep working and witnessing as Paul did. " The wisest thing a man can do when he feels the wheels of his religious being are driving heavily, is to keep himself doggedly to the plain, homely work of daily life." (Read verse 7).

Crispus (verse 8) was one of the very few Paul himself baptised (see 1 Cor. 1. 14). At Corinth he only administered the sacred rite to two ; the " many " who believed and were baptised (verse 8) had the ordinance administered by others.

" **Believed the Lord** " is the R.V. *margin* (verse 8), thus " on " omitted.

Paul Pressed Forward, borne onward by an irresistible impulse. He refused to be self-centred, the great peril of despondency.

A Fine Motto. In an office I saw this timely motto : " When the outlook is not good, try the uplook ! "

BIBLE STUDY

We should search the Scriptures because of a fourfold respect

I. TO ITS AUTHOR ..   .. 2 Peter 1. 21 ; 2 Tim. 3. 16

The Bible is not of human origin. Though written by human hands, its truth came from God. Seeing God has taken so much trouble to provide us with this Book, should I not show sufficient respect to Him by reading and studying it ?

II. TO THE BOOK ITSELF

The oldest known book in the world. The most wonderful volume it has ever seen. Begun by Moses, fifteen centuries before Christ, and finished by John about a century after Christ, it nevertheless is ONE BOOK.

1. **Its Unity is Astonishing.** Not mechanical but organic.
2. **Its Purity is Surprising.** The most majestic thing in all literature.
3. **Its Freshness is Delightful.** Never stale, never dull, sparkling with life.
4. **Its Power and Influence** over men and nations is incalculable.

III. TO ITS READERS

The Bible has been and is still the favourite Book of all classes, learned as well as unlearned. See its immense and ever-increasing circulation. The greatest intellects of all ages have revelled in it, and the wisest have been proud to be known as its students. " We account the Scriptures of God the most sublime philosophy," was the testimony of Newton, the great scientific authority. Therefore should I not take a little trouble to examine the Book that interests and instructs so many of my fellows ?

IV. TO MY OWN LIFE

1. **It is the Instrument of Regeneration** (Jas. 1. 18 ; 1 Peter 1. 23). How can I expect to be born from above if I neglect this instrument ?
2. **Success in Prayer** (Prov. 28. 8) is dependent on a careful study. If I neglect what God has to say to me in His Word, He may turn His ears from what I have to say to Him in prayer.
3. **For Sanctification and Growth** (John 15. 3 ; Eph. 5. 26 ; 1 Peter 2. 23). The Bible is the means for these blessings.

Continued on page 122

GROPING AFTER GOD

Some Illustrations of a Soul Groping and Feeling after God

I. A NEW-BORN BABE

As a new-born child naturally feels after its mother's breast, reaching out its tiny hands in the dark to feel the soft, tender, bountiful bosom.

II. A PLANT OR FLOWER

As plants and flowers grope after the light, turning towards the far away beneficent orb.

III. A BLIND MAN

As a blind man gropes his way along a public street.

IV. A TRAVELLER

As a traveller returning home at night gropes in the dark and cold to find his keyhole.

A Father's Frustrated Purpose. It is pathetic now and again to come across fathers mourning over frustrated purposes and hopes. At great financial sacrifice they have given their sons a first-class education, to fit them for honourable and responsible positions in life, only to find them becoming pedlars, or joining the already over-crowded class known as "unskilled labourers."

"That." We thought of the social failures and family tragedies when pondering upon the wee word "that" in verse 27. Paul points out that God (1) has created us from one common stock (verse 26); (2) marked out our years ("determined the times before appointed"); (3) and geographical position, that is, the place of our birth ("the bounds of their habitation"). And for what purpose? "That" we might seek and find Him, and live in His friendship and love. But instead, man has sought to banish God out of his thought.

Exquisite Thought. What an exquisite thought we have here, that God is brooding over the great races of men; that there never was a nation not dear to Him; that He decides when we are to be born, and where! What a comfort this fact is calculated and intended to be!

Athens. In Paul's time Athens contained the leading University of the world.

Paul's Skill. (1) He begins by complimenting them. Not "superstitious" as A.V. (verse 22), but as in R.V. "religious." "All things I behold bear witness to your carefulness in religion" (C. & H.). (2) He then declares that, instead of being a "setter forth of strange gods" (verse 18), he came to supplement, declaring more fully the nature of the unknown God—(a) Creator (24); (b) too great for human temples (24 and 25); (c) actually engaged in the affairs of this world and our lives (26).

Graphic Phrase. "Might feel after Him" (27), suggesting four specific yet related thoughts, as indicated by the above outline.

MAN'S EXALTED ORIGIN

Some proofs of man's high origin and great dignity

I. PASSION FOR THE INFINITE

Each human being is at times conscious of an unutterable craving for a something or Someone beyond. He possesses reason, intelligence, and something else, best expressed by the word, " Infinite."

II. DESIRE FOR DOMINION

Why do we keep pets ? Not only out of desire for animal companionship, but out of love of dominion. See how man delights to harness nature to the wheels of human progress.

III. THIRST FOR KNOWLEDGE

Man has a passion for knowledge. In some it has been starved until it is very feeble.

IV. APPRECIATION OF BEAUTY

Cattle can move amidst the most beautiful landscape scenes without being touched one bit. Not so man.

V. ADMIRATION OF GOODNESS

Even wicked men revere goodness as they see it in their mothers.

VI. CAPACITY FOR LOVE

In earthly as well as heavenly things.

" **We are the Offspring of God.**" Then are we not by nature the children of God ? Is He not the Universal Father ? If so, what need is there of regeneration ? Not so. In this quotation from the Greek poet Aratus, there is not a word of Fatherhood. The word rendered " offspring " is in the Greek *genos*, a race. The reference is to the Creation work of God, in which He made man in His own likeness. There is no Fatherhood out of Christ. By the use of this word *genos*, Paul meant (a) that man's life is a derived one ; (b) that God is the source of that life ; (c) that man's nature is in some sense akin to His ; (d) that man is God's kinsman, and not child in the evangelical sense. In other words, Paul is emphasising the thought of a common life principle between God and man, and the solidarity of the human race. By natural generation we are His offspring ; by spiritual regeneration His children.

Man's Dignity. Thus he asserts the dignity of man. At other times Paul dwelt on the folly of thinking too highly of self. Here the fault which he finds is that they have taken too low an estimate of their position.

MAN'S TRUE LIFE

To realise our exalted origin should have a definite result in our lives, just as intelligence of princely birth and inheritance would act upon a beggar

I. ASPIRATIONS

1. **The awakening of inborn cravings** and longings (see previous study).
2. **Seeking the full satisfaction** of these longings and cravings by seeking after God.
3. **Realising this can only come** by admission into the family of God by regeneration. The rights of sonship lost by sin can become ours through Christ's redemption.
4. **Desire for the friendship of God** by quick and ready obedience to His will through the fulness of the Holy Spirit.

II. FRIENDS

Desire for better society than the world can offer by making friends of God's children.

III. LIFE

The adornment of attire befitting our exalted origin, viz., holiness of heart and life. "Put on Christ," exhibiting Him in outward life.

IV. WALK

Cultivate a princely walk befitting high rank, carrying oneself with that wonderful blend of dignity and humility which is a true mark of really great ones.

V. SPEECH

Speaking as becometh our high origin, learning well the language of heaven.

VI. ACTIONS

Perform princely deeds, become a worker for God.

Paul's Wisdom. Verse 28 is a quotation from a work by Aratus, a Greek poet of Cilicia, thus a fellow-countryman of Paul. The gracefulness and wisdom of such a quotation deserves notice. In fact, the whole of the discourse reveals Paul's wisdom and tact. It is, of course, not a finished discourse, for the audience broke up at the reference to a Resurrection (note 31 and 32).

" **One Blood** " (verse 26) is in W. " caused to spring from one forefather."

" **Determined the times** " (verse 26) is in W. " And hath...marked out for them an appointed span of life, and the boundaries of their homes, that they might seek God," etc.

How to Live Up to our Exalted Origin. What shall we do if we live up to our exalted origin ? How would a poor working man act if he discovered he was of princely lineage and heir to great wealth ? See above outline.

Attention ! Man, remember you are the work of God. Don't degrade yourself by prostituting your wonderful gifts and powers to inferior uses.

THE MISSING NOTE

Was there a missing note in this great Apostolic Sermon ? Paul did not mention the Central Doctrine of the Death of Christ.

I. ITS IMPORTANCE .. .. .. 1 Cor. 15. 1-4

" First of all " could be rendered, " before all," *i.e.*, first in order of importance.

II. ITS UNIQUENESS

Would you not be shocked if some one on meeting you remarked, " I've got good news for you. ' So-and-so ' is dead." It would be considered bad form to say this even of an enemy. Yet the friends of the Lord Jesus boldly declare Christ's death as good news ! How unique !

III. ITS OFFICIAL ASPECT

Not that " Jesus died," but that " **Christ died.**" Christ is the name of an office. His death was official. He died for our sins.

IV. ITS REALITY

The burial certified the reality of His death.

V. ITS SUFFICIENCY

Christ's Resurrection proved the all-sufficiency of His death.

What is the Gospel ? What is your answer ? Please give it in the very words of Scripture. Turn to 1 Corinthians 15. 1 to 4.

The Missing Note. Do you detect a missing Gospel note in Paul's Mars' Hill sermon ? Connect 1 Cor. 2. 2 with 1 Cor. 3. 1, and in the light of Heb. 6. 1. In *The King's Writ* a writer has declared : "It is evident that Paul felt that he had failed at Athens. His sermon on Mars' Hill was conciliatory learned, interesting, and edifying. But he had not given that prominence to the Cross in his message that he was accustomed to give, and that he ought to have given. He set the Cross into the shade ; the word of the Cross was not emphasised ; and hence, as he well knew, his failure to evangelise. He had carried his conciliation too far... The Resurrection was spoken of, and the Judgment was spoken of, but not the Cross. He was addressing philosophers, and he addressed them with that wisdom of words, in a manner that he afterwards depreciated in 1 Corinthians."

Uniqueness. Of all the millions of deaths, the *only* death that ever became Gospel or Glad Tidings was Christ's death on Calvary.

Did Paul Fail ? Note verses 32-34. Some mocked, some procrastinated, and some believed. Was not that the same result as in other places ? See 13. 45, 48 ; 14. 4 ; 17. 4, 5, etc. And is not this still the result of the preaching of the Word ?

PREACHING — I

As a result of the study of Paul's Mars' Hill Address, which brings out the importance of right preaching, a detailed study on preaching is timely

I. WHAT IS PREACHING ?
Four definitions are given by Dr. Young.

1. To Bring or Tell Good Tidings.
(a) BRING—by books, letters, or tracts, " The *words* of the preacher " (Eccles. 1. 1).
(b) TELL—by speech.

2. To Tell or Announce Thoroughly
(a) Adapt voice to size of building or audience.
(b) Clear speaking more effective than loud speaking.

3. To Talk
(a) In the view of Scripture, individual, and personal dealing is preaching (Acts 8. 35). " *Opened* his mouth." Don't speak through an almost closed mouth
(b) This definition suggests conversational preaching. " Preaching is dignified conversation." This is the meaning of the word " admonish " in Rom. 15. 14, " able to bear personal testimony."

4. To Teach (Luke 20. 1)
(a) Two distinct gifts are in in this Scripture.
(b) Our Lord combined both in His preaching.
(c) " Do the work of an evangelist." Do not neglect this gift. Yet let your preaching be a teaching preaching.
(d) This suggests *informative* preaching, giving to others what has been blessed to your own soul. " Preaching is the bringing of truth through personality."

II. WHERE TO PREACH
1. To an audience of one (Acts 8. 35).
2. To the Poor (Matt. 11. 5).
3. To the Great Congregation (Psa. 40. 9).
4. In Cities (Matt. 11. 1).
5. In Towns (Mark 1. 38).
6. In Villages (Acts 8. 25).
7. In " Regions beyond you " (2 Cor. 10. 16).
8. Everywhere (Mark 16. 20).

III. WHAT TO PREACH.
1. We are not left to choose (Jonah 3. 2).

Continued on page 123

PREACHING — II

Having considered What is Preaching ? Where to Preach, and What to Preach, we complete the Subject in this Study.

IV. THEMES TO PREACH

Each theme associated with the vicarious death, never apart from it.

1. **The Humanity of Christ.**
   (a) Declared by His Name, Jesus (Acts 8. 35 ; 17. 3).
   (b) Its reality is cheering to us (see John 4. 6, etc.).
2. **The Lordship of Jesus.**
   (a) This Jesus is Christ (Acts 17. 3).
   (b) Christ Jesus the Lord (2 Cor. 4. 5).
   It is the Deity of Jesus which gives value and efficacy to His death.
3. **The Glory of Christ** (Psa. 29. 9 ; 145. 6).
4. **The Benefits of His Atoning Death.** The value of doctrinal preaching.
   (a) The Word of Faith (Rom. 10. 8).
   (b) Repentance (Matt. 4. 17).
   (c) Forgiveness (Acts 13. 38).
   (d) Peace (Rom. 10. 15).
   (e) Righteousness (Psa. 40. 9 ; 2 Peter 2. 5).
   (f) His lovingkindness and truth (Psa. 40. 10).
   (g) Deliverance (Luke 4. 18).
5. **Doctrine and Christ.** Note, " Jesus *and* the resurrection " (Acts 17. 18 ; 4. 2 ; 5. 42). " *Through* this Man " (Acts 13. 38). Be on your guard. In your desire to give doctrinal addresses, never preach doctrine apart from Christ. Let your Saviour and His substitutionary death ever be the centre and sum of all doctrine.

V. WHO SHOULD PREACH ?

1. **Sent Ones** (Rom. 10. 15). He cannot *send* those who have not *come* to Him, or who have not been sitting or standing before Him.
2. **Anointed Ones** (Isa. 61. 1 ; Luke 4. 18).

VI. HOW TO PREACH

Not with a stiff neck (Psa. 75. 5).

1. **Humbly**, but not apologetically. Yours is the King's Message.
2. **Conversationally,** *i.e.*, in a homely fashion. It is a Personal Message.
3. **Manly**, confidently (Rom. 1. 16).

OUR VALUE

In Four Ways we can Discover Man's Value to God.

I. BY COST OF PRODUCTION

If an article is produced only at great cost of energy, time, and labour, one may rest assured it must be of value. Genesis 1. 26, 27 tells us that man was produced as the result of a distinctive creative act of God, following consultation of the Divine Trinity.

II. BY COST OF PURCHASE

Generally the value of anything is tested by its purchase price. To create man took more trouble than to create a universe. To redeem fallen man God had to part with His All.

III. BY COST OF SECURING

Many people have money in Chancery, yet, although they can produce every legal proof, do not trouble to secure it, because the legal expenses would amount to more than the sum in question. If one is willing to part with all one's time and possessions to secure an inheritance, that is proof of its value to them. The salvation of every soul costs months and sometimes years of patient labour on the part of the Holy Spirit. How valuable we must be.

IV. BY CARE BESTOWED IN KEEPING

The value of anything may be gauged by the precautions taken to secure its safety. If we see an owner careful to put and keep in a strong safe some article, we know it is of value to him. What trouble the Lord takes over the preservation of His own jewels !

Our Value to God. Boswell, who was practising as a barrister in Scotland, wrote Dr. Johnson to say that he was coming to London to plead as an advocate in an important case. In his reply, the old Dr. said : " I think nothing more likely to make your life pass happily away *than the consciousness of your own value,* which eminence in your profession will certainly confer." Brief life is here our portion. How can it pass happily ? By discovering we are of value, to man certainly, but supremely to God.

Illustration in Everyday Life. If a *workman* imagines he is of no value to his master, his services will become a weariness, and worse. He will lose heart, become careless, and cease to be of any value. If we think our *neighbours* and friends think little of our usefulness, we become despondent, and practically useless.

" **Can a Man be Profitable to God** " was asked by Eliphaz (Job 22. 2). It was left unanswered in the Old Testament. The answer in the New Testament is threefold :

(*a*) Man, once profitable to God, through sin had become unprofitable

Continued on page 123

RESURRECTION

I. OF THE DEAD .. .. Acts 17. 32

Though the heathen nations knew of the endlessness
of man, that is the immortality of the soul, they never
dreamt of the resurrection of the body. This was a
truth well known to the Jews, even as far back as
Job (19. 25).

II. FROM THE DEAD .. .. Phil. 3. 11 (R.V.)

Though the Jews knew of the resurrection *of* the dead,
they never imagined a resurrection *from* the dead,
until this was revealed by God to Paul. This takes
place when the Lord comes back *for* His own. The
exact period between the first and second resurrec-
tions is one thousand years (Rev. 20. 5).

The Dignity of Man. " Man, so small, so tiny, that from yonder hill-
top he appears but as a speck in the valley below, yet within him the roar
of the infinite sea of Eternity is for ever sounding. Just as a man will
pick up a shell from the seashore, and carry it three thousand miles inland,
and listening, he hears the beating music of the waves that made it ; so,
oh man, no matter how far thou hast wandered from God, in thy heart is
a passion of Deity the sounding of the billows of Eternity " (Campbell
Morgan).

God Winking (verse 70). It is a curious phrase, sounding rather strange
to us. Look at Leviticus 20. 4. " Hide their eyes " in our version, is
" winked " in the Septuagint. It means " overlooked," *forbearance, not
connivance.*

The Resurrection of the body was a doctrine entirely unknown to the
wisest of the heathen, so no wonder some " mocked " (verse 32) and others,
being a little more polite, adopted a nicer and more popular way of getting
rid of him. " We will hear thee again of this matter."

A Great Question. " If a man die shall he live again ? " (Job. 14. 14).
Only a short sentence of eight single syllabled words, yet one of the greatest.
Job's question waited long for an answer. Weary centuries rolled by.
At last the question asked by the Old Testament man of sorrows, is
answered by the New Testament Man of Sorrows—" Though he were
dead, yet shall he live " (John 11. 25 and 26).

PAUL DESPONDENT

Paul was " oppressed in the spirit " (verse 5), or, as the Arabic version renders it, " Grief beset the spirit of Paul." Why ?

I. HE WAS ALONE
And in a strange city. Solitude is a hard trial to sensitive natures such as Paul's, who was constantly craving for human companionship.

II. HE HAD NO MONEY
And so had to hire himself out as a tent-maker.

III. HE WAS NOT WELL 17. 15
Owing to blurred vision he had to be led.

IV. HE WAS OVERWORKED   ..   ..   1 Cor. 9. 15
Working hard at tent-making all day long, and preaching in his spare time.

V. HE WAS PERSECUTED   ..   ..   verse 6 (R.V.)
" Opposed and *railed*."

VI. HIS WORK SEEMED A FAILURE.
Judged from human standards.

VII. HE WAS BURDENED
On behalf of the Churches.

VIII. HE SAW ABOUNDING INIQUITY
On every hand.

Two Renderings. " Paul was *pressed in spirit* " (verse 5, A.V.) ; " Paul was *constrained by the Word* " (R.V.). There is a vast difference between these two renderings. In the A.V., Paul is *pressed down*, in the R.V. he is *pressed forward*. In the former the apostle is depressed, in the latter he is the enthusiast, constrained by the Word, focusing all his efforts on the proving of Jesus' Deity and Messiaship.

Which True ? Now, which of these renderings is correct ? Suppose we take them both as in this study and the next ? " But both cannot be right," you say. Do not be in too great a hurry. There is Scripture to show that the great apostle to the Gentiles was very much depressed at this time, and in this place.

Circumstances. He left Athens and came to Corinth (18. 1). He hired himself to a master tent maker, and was used of God to both his conversion and that of his wife (see Outlined Romans, page 101). In his Synagogue ministry in his spare time he appealed to *reason* (verse 4).

The Testimony of the Two Letters to the Thessalonians. It is generally understood that 1 Thessalonians was written between verses 5 and 6, and 2 Thessalonians between 11 and 12. How does the apostle describe in those letters his feelings before the return of the two brethren from Thessalonica ? He speaks of " all our distresses and affliction " (1 Thess. 3. 7). He tells them he was tortured by anxiety concerning them (2 Thess. 7. 5 and 6). He wrote afterwards to the Corinthians. How does he describe his feelings ? (see 1 Cor. 2. 3).

What ? The great apostle depressed and cast down ! Ah ! he was only human. Note 2 Cor. 1. 8 ; 2. 1, 4, 13 ; 4. 8 and 9 ; 6. 10. What a help this is to all of us.

GALLIO

Gallio was careless and indifferent. What were the mistaken notions behind his conduct ?

I. ACTIONS BEFORE IDEAS

He cared not for ideas, but for actions. He was a busy man, a man of affairs. Busy men are apt to value action more than thought. Yet all the great things in life, buildings, statues, pictures, were once only thoughts in the minds of architects, sculptors, or artists.

II. CONDUCT BEFORE DOCTRINE

He cared not for doctrine, but for conduct. He thought religion had nothing to do with conduct. Perhaps he thought this to be a squabble about empty superstitions.

III. WANTED NO RELIGION

He cared for no religion in particular. Probably as a Stoic, he viewed them all as right.

One Act. " Cared for none of these things " (verse 17). As long as the world lasts, Gallio will be known by this statement. His very name now is synonymous for philosophical indifference. Is it not strange how immortality comes to some. One solitary act in history is recorded to most. How little Gallio dreamed that he would live for ever in men's minds by reason of this one judicial act of indifference.

Events. Paul spent eighteen months teaching the Word of God at Corinth (verse 11). A new Governor was appointed (verse 12). Gallio was brother of Seneca, and Seneca was Nero's tutor. We know he was usually amiable and popular. His brother speaks of him as loved by all.

A Surprise. Paul's enemies received a shock. As amiability and firmness do not usually go together, the enemies of Paul thought they had a fine chance of getting rid of him, so " brought him to the Judgment seat " (verse 12). Paul was about to defend himself when Gallio stopped and dismissed the case. They seemed unwilling to go, as he had to use force and " drave them " (verse 16).

Tables Turned. Evidently the Greek populace favoured Paul, and resented the conduct of his Jewish enemies, for they seized the new Jewish Synagogue official who had taken the place of Crispus (verses 8 and 17). Probably this new official was subsequently converted (see 1. Cor. 1. 1 and 2).

The Don't Cares. The very name of Gallio has become a by-word. He stands before us as a type of the indifferent and careless ones, as representing the " Don't Cares," a very large class indeed.

Paul at Corinth. (1) His humble beginning (1-3) ; (2) His regular service (4-7) ; (3) Its happy results (8) ; (4) The Lord's encouragement and exhortations (9-11) ; (5) His conflict with the Jews (12, 13) ; (6) His rescue by the Greeks (14-17).

SEMI-CHRISTIAN

There was something lacking in experience of Apollos.

I. NOT KNOWLEDGE .. .. verse 24

It was not the lack of the Word, for he was steeped in a knowledge of the Word of God, "Mighty in the Scriptures," and skilled in the use of them. This knowledge was lodged in his intellect by catechetical instruction, as the marginal note indicates, "taught by word of mouth."

II. NOT SPEECH .. .. verse 24

For he had an eloquent tongue to convey the truth.

III. NOT NATURE .. .. verse 25

For he had an ardent, industrious nature. He was "fervent in spirit." But zeal and enthusiasm alone are not sufficient.

IV. NOT SERVICE .. .. verse 25

For he was honoured in his ministry, "the things of the Lord."

V. BUT EXPERIENCE

He had not experienced a personal Pentecost. His defect was not in theology, but in a vital point of experience. He had been born of the Spirit, but was not filled with the Spirit.

Erasmus. The heading of this page is borrowed from the great scholar, Erasmus. Concerning the eloquent Alexandrian, he writes : " *Hic Apollos erat semo Christianus* " i.e., this Apollos was a semi-Christian. Apollos, alas, is a representative of hosts of professed disciples of Christ to-day.

Analyse. That being so, let us analyse his character, and ascertain what it possessed and lacked. It is startling to find how far he went, and yet lacked. This should cause us to search our hearts.

Events. Leaving Corinth, he embarked at Ephesus for Antioch, thus ending his second great missionary journey. At verse 23 he began his third journey, which lasted four years.

ACCURACY

Of the need of accuracy there is no need to dwell, but consider some of the things it is well to be accurate in

I. IN SCRIPTURE STUDY .. .. .. Luke 1. 3

Many were the unsuccessful attempts to write our Lord's life (Luke 1. 1). But Luke claims more *accurate* knowledge (for "perfect" read "accurately").

1. As the result of personal investigation.
2. As the result of inspiration " from above."

This shows that an accurate knowledge of the Word of God can only be secured by earnest endeavour plus Divine help.

II. IN TEACHING .. .. .. Acts 18. 25, 26

In the teaching of the Scriptures. Here is seen a delicate regard for the feelings of another. They invited Apollos to a private interview in the seclusion of their own humble home, and with the utmost respect for his standing and attainment, and there politely enlightened him.

III. IN OBEDIENCE (circumspectly; lit., accurately) Eph. 5.15

How careful some tutors are concerning the deportment of their pupils. How careful we ought to be to *walk* accurately, never separating doctrine and practice.

IV. IN ADVENT TRUTH .. .. .. 1 Thess. 5. 2

Their accuracy in advent truth was owing to Paul's clear instruction whilst he was there.

" **Perfectly.**" The word " perfectly," found several times in the Word, is literally " accurately." By a study of these as above, we get a series of important truths.

" **Believed through Grace** " (verse 27). What an exquisite phrase!

THE HOLY SPIRIT

Two questions are suggested by Paul's words in verse 2 as to the work of the Holy Spirit in the heart

I. AT CONVERSION

What Ministry of the Holy Spirit took place when you first believed ? "Did ye receive the Holy Spirit when ye believed ? " (verse 2, R.V.).

1. Are you a Believer? What a lovely name for Christians!
2. Have you ever endeavoured to ascertain what you received then ?
3. You were then regenerated by the Spirit. Were you filled ?
4. That is the ideal conversion, regenerated by and filled with the Spirit at the same time.
5. These believers now received the Divine fulness (verse 6), and their progress in Divine things was wonderful, so much so, that they could understand so splendid a letter as was sent them later (Ephesians).

II. SINCE CONVERSION

What Ministry of the Holy Spirit has taken place since you believed ? "Have ye received the Holy Ghost since ye believed ? " (A.V.).

1. The gift of the fulness of the Holy Spirit needs to be renewed day by day.
2. What a blunder it is to live on a past experience !
3. He desires to anoint us each morning with *fresh* oil.

Puzzled. Sometimes botanists and geologists are puzzled over new specimens discovered, and cannot rest until they have named them. The apostle in his travels kept his promise by again visiting Ephesus (17. 21), and there discovered an altogether new and puzzling type of believers.

He Noted (1) They were "disciples" (verse 1) ; (2) "the men were about twelve" (curious phrase) (verse 7) ; (3) had been baptised (verse 3) ; yet powerless, joyless, lacking in spirituality.

Significance of Paul's question was that he missed in them the marks of the Spirit. They were John's disciples, living in ignorance of the history and experience of Pentecost.

John. This is the last reference to John the Baptist in the New Testament.

Opinions Differ as to the exact nature of Paul's question. Both the A.V. and R.V. renderings convey helpful lessons.

Step Forward. A gentleman wanted to try a new shower bath. He turned a tap which he thought would produce a shower of water. Nothing however happened. He tried repeatedly and then gave up in despair. Before next morning he made inquiries, and found that, in addition to turning the tap, *he should have immediately stepped forward* on to the board immediately under the spray which released a spring. It is not enough to pray, we must step forward in faith.

THE BONFIRE

The steps that led to this notable bonfire (verse 19)

I. BELIEVING .. .. verse 18

In verse 9 some would not believe. Believing implies a definite act of the will.

II. CONFESSING .. .. verse 18

A careful study of this verse leads to the conclusion that many had been believers for some time, and had secretly practised these arts. The judgment on the seven brothers (verse 16) roused into activity their consciences.

III. FORSAKING .. .. verse 19

According to their estimation, these books were worth more than £2000 in our money.

IV. REWARDED

They lost money but gained peace. As recompense for the destruction of bad books, they received a rich present of three good ones—Ephesians, John, Revelation. These three books were written specially for them.

Savonarola. Readers of Savonarola's biography will remember a similar scene in Venice, when men and women, artists and musicians, brought the things in which they most delighted in, and burnt them before St. Mark's.

Paul's Great Opportunity. Dr. Liddon points out that the greatest opportunity of Paul's life was perhaps his teaching for two years in the school of Tyrannus (verse 9).

"**That Way**" (verse 9). The Christian doctrine called a "way," a road, more than a body of truth.

"**God Wrought**" (verse 11). Paul was only the channel. He ever gave God the glory.

"**The Name**" (verse 13). Suggestive. Shows that Paul did all in that precious Name.

Ephesian Letters. Ephesus was the head-quarters of magical art. All sorts of charms and incantations were devised and sold there. Mysterious symbols or monograms called "Ephesian Letters" were written here and sold as charms. The study of these symbols was an elaborate science. Books, both numerous and costly, were compiled for its professors. These were the books that were burned.

1 Corinthians was written at this time.

Question. Are there any books on your book shelves that trouble your conscience ? Surely they ought to be burned !

TRADE OUR POLITICS

Demetrius's speech was clever and crafty

I. HIS WORKMEN

He addressed first his own workmen, then others similarly engaged (verse 23, w.).

II. LOSS OF TRADE

He lightly touched upon the loss of trade, but did not dwell on that topic too long. Though the natural man is intensely selfish by nature, he does not like to be told so too openly (verse 25).

III. THEIR RELIGION

He dwelt mostly upon an imagined concern for their religion. This speech is a perfect example of how self-interest can masquerade in the garb of pure concern for lofty objects. Yet, see how it betrayed itself.

A Mighty Urge. Success at Ephesus did not lead to forgetfulness of his commission, nor of the need of other regions (verse 21). With this mighty urge on him, he sent two of his companions as forerunners, " but he himself stayed in Asia for a season " (verse 22).

Trade Union Riot. But a Trade Union riot hastened his departure.

A New Antagonism. This narrative reveals a new phase of antagonism to the Gospel, a kind of Trade Union demonstration.

" **Great is Diana of the Ephesians** " (verse 28 and 34). This cry has been found inscribed on altars and tablets, showing it was a kind of watchword in that district. Note, the mob kept howling this for two hours.

Mob Muddle. With a touch of scorn the historian describes the muddle the mob was in when they desired to make a charge (verse 32).

A Solemn Fact. Is not this a fact, that in our country there are some trades which would be wiped out if Christ's laws of life were universally adopted ?

EXPERIENCES

Many and varied experiences are touched on in these few verses

I. MUCH EXHORTATION .. .. verse 2

His soul was burdened on their account. So much to say, and so little time to say it.

II. MUCH PERSECUTION .. .. verse 3

The enemies of the Gospel were pugnacious and persistent, following the apostle wherever he went.

III. MUCH PREACHING .. .. verse 7

1. Even the apostles at times preached long sermons.
2. This service must have lasted seven hours.

IV. MUCH TALKING .. .. verse 11

Out of the fulness of his heart.

V. MUCH COMFORT .. .. verse 12

Eutychus was raised to life, and Paul resumed his journey.

Paul's Departure. After the uproar, Paul had a touching interview with the Ephesian believers, and departed for Macedonia.

Three Months in Greece (verse 2). No particulars are given of that three months' mission. We know 2 Corinthians was written during that time. Probably between verses 3 and 4 the Epistles to the Galatians and the Romans were written.

Seven Days at Troas (as verse 6).

Godly Habit. Verse 7 points out the regular custom of Believers on " First Day."

A Defence of Eutychus. (a) A Sunday School Teacher asked her class : " What does the story of Eutychus teach ? " and a girl promptly replied : " That ministers should not preach too long sermons." Was she right ? (b) This man was " young," probably too young to be interested in Paul's address, as all the others gladly listened to Paul all night. (c) Probably an ill-ventilated room, crowded to excess, with smell from " many lights " (verse 8).   (d) It was an upstairs room, and in consequence hot with the sun and more difficult to ventilate.

COMMUNION

I. WHAT ?

Communion is the interchange between the Lord and the individual believer.

II. WHERE ?

1. **At the Mercy Seat** (Exod. 25. 22), *i.e.*, the place of the blood sprinkling.
2. **On your bed** (Psa. 4. 4).
3. **Along life's way** (Luke 24. 15 ; Acts 20. 13).
4. **Anywhere and everywhere.**

III. HOW ?

The two chief conditions of communion with God are :

1. Resort to and conscious dependence on **the Blood** (1 Cor. 10. 16).
2. **Oneness,** affinity, a heart right with Him (2 Cor. 6. 14).

The Value of Solitude. The journey on foot from Troas to Assos is about twenty miles. Seeing he could make that journey by ship, and noting that his companions sailed, we ask, why did Paul, who loved earthly companionship, go alone ? He was longing for solitude for communion with God, such solitude as was impossible in the crowded quarters on board ship. There was *a twenty miles walk with God*, in order to secure spiritual refreshment and communion.

"**Interchange between Him and me.**" Dr. Fullerton, in his biography of Dr. F. B. Meyer, writes : " The day before he died, when, in response to a question as to whether he then had any new vision of his Saviour, looking upward he simply said, ' No, just the constant interchange between Him and me.' Interchange—the word is worthy of remembrance— not prayer only, nor only worship, but fellowship, the speech of the heart and the response of the Spirit." Could we have a finer description of communion between the Lord and His people !

A Sixfold Analysis of our approach to God. (*a*) *Prayer*, the presentation of a petition. (*b*) *Supplication*, adding to the petition a promise from His Word, and pleading it. (*c*) *Intercession*, pleading for others. (*d*) *Giving of Thanks* (see 1 Tim. 2. 1). (*e*) *Communion*, interchange between the Lord and His child. (*f*) *Worship*, prostration and adoration of the believer before His Lord.

SERVICE

Some of the conditions of serving the Lord, as illustrated in the character and life of Paul

I. CONSTANT .. .. verse 18

" **At all seasons.**" In season and out of season, when the mood was on him and when it was not. Constantly. What a word that is !

II. HUMBLE .. .. verse 19

"**With all humility of mind.**" That is to say, not a mock humility ; not the outward appearance of humility without the inward reality. Humility is the prince of virtues.

III. UNDAUNTED .. .. verse 19

1. **Tears.** Paul was not ashamed that it should be known that sometimes he went forth weeping, bearing precious seed. His tears were the sign of his earnestness.

2. **Testings.** Though tested and tried in many ways.

3. **Dangers.** He truly " counted his life not dear unto him."

IV. FAITHFUL .. .. verse 20

" **I kept nothing back.**" The bitter as well as the sweet. Painful as well as palatable truths. Not merely his favourite subjects, but " the whole counsel of God." (Note verse 27).

V. DILIGENT .. .. verse 20

1. Public preaching.

2. Private visiting. (See next study.)

Parting Address at Miletus. This parting address to the Ephesian elders is perfect in simplicity, pathos, and dignity. In it we find love without weakness, personal reference without egotism, tenderness and yet solemnity wonderfully blended.

Personal Testimony. Here he gives his personal testimony. Not in an arrogant, self-satisfied, or self-assertive spirit does he refer to his past services. The hearers were only too conscious of the truth of every word.

" **Serving the Lord.**" What a common phrase this is in His Holy Book. Yet how full of meaning.

A CITY MISSIONARY

Paul might be described as the First City Missionary, going
" from house to house " in Ephesus for two years

I. EXPLANATION   ..   ..   *" Shewed."*

He was careful to ascertain if his ministry and messages
were fully understood. He made certain that they
fully grasped it.

II. TEACHING ..   ..   *" Taught."*

Privately as well as publicly, to the one as well as to
large congregations. His was a teaching as well as
a preaching ministry.

III. TESTIMONY   ..   ..   *" Testifying."*

He not only preached and taught, but mingled both
with personal testimony. The meaning of the word
is to "attest earnestly," putting his whole soul into
his words.

First City Missionary. What is known as City Mission methods were
first clearly practised by the Apostle Paul during his two years' work at
Ephesus.

Conversational Evangelism. Conversational evangelism is the pattern
service our Lord has set for us. Whilst He ministered to the crowds,
preaching successfully in an entirely, new, original. and powerful manner,
yet He never undervalued the audiences of one. Individual work was
recognised and practised by Him as of first-rate importance. He got into
close quarters with the various individuals He encountered in His daily
pilgrimages. The fullest and frankest revelations of Himself were given
to audiences of one.

House-to-House Work. But, as far as we know, our Lord was not able
to visit the homes of the people *consecutively*. He was frequently a guest,
but so great were the crowds following Him that His short three and a half
years of public ministry was occupied mainly in public preaching, with
occasional private ministry. But during Paul's two years' ministry in the
City of Ephesus, in addition to public work, he systematically and consecutively visited the homes of the people for definite personal evangelism,
the work that City Missions were called into being to do just a century ago.

His Message. (a) Repentance—toward God ; (b) Faith—toward the
Lord Jesus. A much neglected message.

UNMOVABLE

" None of these things move me," was Paul's cheerful antici-
pation of future suffering

I. WHAT THINGS ?

   1. **Uncertainty** (verse 22). " Not knowing."
   2. **Divine Warning** (verse 23). " The Holy Ghost wit-
nesseth."
     (*a*) Of Imprisonment.
     (*b*) Of Suffering.
   3. **Repeated Solicitations** (verse 23). " In every city."
Not in one or two isolated places.
   4. **Human Entreaty** (21. 4, 10-13).

II. WHY ?

   1. **Divine Impulse.** " From an impulse which we cannot
resist " (verse 22, 20 c.).
   2. **Sacrificial Spirit.** " Neither count I my life dear unto
myself " (verse 24).

Was Paul Wrong ? Regarding Paul's last recorded journey to Jerusalem, God's people everywhere and at all times have held a variety of
opinions. Repeated warnings were given him of its hazardous nature by
his own loving friends, and it is clearly acknowledged that they were so
moved by the Holy Spirit. Was he wrong in disregarding such intima-
tions ? Was he misled by his own ardent spirit ? Did he foolishly and
unnecessarily risk his life ? If not, then why did the Holy Ghost seek to
dissuade him through his own loving friends ? Or were those warnings
only testings, like Abram who was commanded to offer his only son,
to see if he would risk all for the love he had for his Lord ? One scholar
who leans to this view, writes : " His friends did not think so. 'When he
would not be persuaded, we ceased, saying, *The Will of the Lord be done.*'
The multiplied warnings of the Spirit were intended to prepare the apostle
for all that might befall him ; but when he took the hazard, and dared the
worst that the enemies of his Lord could do, we may believe that his great
Master accepted the sacrifice. St. Paul's courageous decision was joyfully
determined on " for the sake of the Name."

How should we treat friends when *they refuse to follow our advice* ? Do
not scold, sulk, criticise, or denounce ; just do as Paul's friends did (see
verse 14).

" In the Spirit " (verse 22). Cp. Acts 21. 4. " In Acts 20. 22, Paul's
own spirit is meant ; in 21. 4 the Holy Spirit. Paul's motive in going to
Jerusalem seems to have been his great affection for the Jews (Rom. 9.
1-5), and his hope that the gifts of the Gentile Churches, sent through him
to poor saints in Jerusalem (Rom. 15. 25-28), would open the hearts of the
law-bound Jewish believers to the Gospel of the Grace of God " (*Scofield
Bible Note*).

THE GOAL

How to Finish our Course with Joy

I. ATTITUDE ..   .. verse 21

A Right Attitude toward God and to Christ. Get right with God and the Lord Jesus. Repentance and faith.

II. ESTIMATION   ..   .. verse 24

A Right Estimation of Life. Life as a " race," not a pastime or a holiday. Racing requires effort, determination, concentration, self-denial.

III. SPHERE ..   .. verse 24

A Right Sphere to Live Within. A racecourse. Life as a race on *a specified course.*

IV. DECISION ..   .. verse 24

A Right Decision to Take. Immovability, steadfastly, continuing in His will.

V. SELF ..   .. verse 24

A Right View of Self. A life of self-sacrifice. " Not I, but Christ."

VI. TRUTH ..   .. verses 20, 27

A Right Treatment of Truth. Declaring all the counsel of God.

VII. CONSCIENCE   ..   .. verse 26

A Right Good Conscience, that can even call man to witness.

VIII. SPIRIT ..   .. verse 24

A Right Spirit. " With joy."

Aspiration and Realisation. Paul's *aspiration* is shown in Acts 20. 24 ; his *realisation*, 2 Timothy 4. 7.

" **With Joy** " (verse 24). A devout scholar writes : " These words, ' with joy,' are omitted by the Revisers, but Ewald and other scholars insist that they should be received as part of the true text. In many cases the phrase is Pauline. Though he passed through a tempest of affliction, he was always radiant and rejoicing. Christ had made him very glad, and all earth's sufferings could not quench his joy."

THE FATHER'S SORROW

The Sacrifice and Sorrow of God the Father was that of—

I. LOVE

It has been finely said that when a nation sends forth her sons to war, the keenest pain is not felt by the men who, amidst much excitement, march through the streets or face the enemy in battle. The costliest sacrifice is that of the wives and mothers, who wait and watch and pray with passive agony.

II. FORESIGHT

Mortal man cannot foretell the sorrows and sufferings awaiting loved ones. But the sufferings of the Son of God lay as a burden and a sorrow and a sacrifice on the heart of God the Father from the foundation of the world.

III. SIGHT

When our soldiers first went to war the suffering of those left behind was great; but how much greater if they had been passive observers of their loved one's danger, or sorrow, or suffering. The Father saw all, and so felt all.

IV. PARENTAL CHASTISER

Children find it hard to believe that their parents feel the blows inflicted far more than they do. Yet it is a fact. It was God the Father who sacrificed His Son. " It pleased the Lord to bruise Him."

Moving. Paul's address to the Ephesian elders is one of the most moving addresses in the Bible. It throbs with emotion. Memories of the past crowd upon his mind.

From Himself. In the first portion of his speech he dwells upon himself (verses 18-27); first looking *backwards* with grateful humility, and then looking *forward* with cheerful Christian courage. In the second section (28-35) he turns from himself and his work to that of the elders. The care of the Ephesian Church must now be theirs, as it no longer can be his : for this they had been designated by the Holy Spirit (verse 28).

To Feed. " Flock " is an Old Testament emblem for the people of God. "Feed," *i.e.*, pasture. To be made an Overseer by the world is to be made a master ; but to be created Overseer by the Holy Spirit is to be made a servant—not overseers so much to rule as to feed.

"God—which He Purchased with His Own Blood " (verse 28). How daring and startling is this statement. Most assuredly this declares the Deity of Christ. God was in Christ. But there is another thought: Cannot a father, whose son has been wounded or slain in battle say, " My blood has been shed on the battlefield ? " The part the Father took in the great work of Christ on the Cross has been much neglected. Surely it was only in agony that Abraham prepared to offer his son. Both suffered. If the visible sacrifice on the Cross was Christ's, the invisible sacrifice was God's. Note the Father's sorrow in above outline.

GIVING

Some of the reasons why it is more blessed to give than to receive

I. ABILITY
To be in a position to give is the result of God's blessing.

II. SPIRIT
To give to others in the right spirit is to give to Him: " Inasmuch."

III. EXAMPLE
It is following our great Exampler, who gave His all in giving His only begotten Son.

IV. APPROVAL
The Lord's benediction is specially upon the benevolent and generous.

V. CONSCIENCE
The treasure of an approved conscience is ours when we give in His Name.

VI. REWARD
Giving down here is laying up treasure in Heaven.

Beside God. " I commend you to God " is literally, " I lay you down beside God."

The True and False. In verse 33 lieth one great difference between the true and the false.

Unrecorded. In verse 35 we have one of our Lord's utterances unrecorded in the Gospels. It is a sentiment worthy of Christ. It is a golden saying, snatched from oblivion. " Remember "—this indicates they had heard it before.

Condition. It must be the giving of those who have first given themselves (see 2 Cor. 8. 5).

David Hill (Wesleyan Missionary in China). To build a chapel, his own father sent £500. This generous gift greatly touched and gladdened the son's heart, and he speaks repeatedly of it in letters and journals. The father himself esteemed it lightly, and to a friend he said that *"the greatest gift he ever gave to China was David himself; everything else was easy after that."*

Lesson. (1) God the Father's greatest gift—Son—everything else easy and given through that gift.

(2) When I have given myself, other things become easy to give.

REJECTED ADVICE

The Valuable Lessons from Paul's Rejection of Advice

I. GOD OVERRULES .. .. .. verses 19, 20

A striking example of how the Lord can overrule the errors of His people for His glory and for the good of His cause. Was Paul wrong in going to Jerusalem ? Was he headstrong and self-willed ? Commenting on verse 4, one has said : " The prediction was of the Spirit, the prohibition was their own." If Paul was in error, we see how God overruled it.

II. DEVOTION TO DUTY .. .. verse 13

A splendid example of courageous devotion to duty, of rigid adherence to the path of duty. A striking blending of melting tenderness and iron determination. God had told him to go to Jerusalem, though warning him what to expect there.

III. REJECTED ADVICE .. .. verse 14

A useful hint as to what to do when our well-meant advice is disregarded. Be resigned and commend to the Lord. This attitude was—

1. **Splendid**, and a fine example for us to follow.
2. **Sensible**. After all, what else could they do to a man who was unmoved even by tears.

" **Gotten** " **Away** (verse 1) is in W., " Torn themselves away," a graphic phrase.

Log. In the first three verses we have extracts from the log of the voyage. It shows the leisurely way of navigation in those days. Evidently they sailed into harbour each evening.

" **Finding** " (verse 4) is " Having *searched* " in W.

Philip. Twenty years have passed since Philip was last mentioned (Acts 8). Evidently, with his family, he had settled in Caesarea (verse 8). " Here is a beautiful instance of the contented acceptance of a lot very much less conspicuous, very much less brilliant than the early beginnings had seemed to promise."

Agabus. Fourteen years had passed since he had last appeared on the scene (Acts 11. 28).

AN EARLY DISCIPLE

I. FROM THE COUNTRY

Mnason was a city dweller from the country, a Jew with a Greek name, born on Gentile soil, Cyprus, the same place from which Barnabas came.

II. AN EARLY DISCIPLE

He was one of the primitive band of disciples, perhaps one of the seventy, attracted to the Lord during His early ministry.

III. LOYAL TO CONVICTIONS

He was loyal to his earliest convictions, he had held fast to his early faith.

IV. HUMBLE

He did not despise either the company or the service of younger Christians, for Paul was his junior by some years. The younger did not despise his company. Youthful ardour and experience of the aged is a useful blend.

V. SERVED

Though living an obscure life, he did what he could. Only two things said of him—that he was an early disciple and that he entertained. He may not have possessed eloquence or genius, but he did open his house for Paul and his company, thus taking a share in their work.

Early. Instead of "old disciples," R.V. gives "early disciple." It seems but a very slight and unimportant alteration, yet it is a significant change. "Old" and "early" are not quite the same. Mnason was both old—advanced in years—and early—a disciple from the beginning, one of the original group of believers who had seen and followed Christ.

After those Days (verse 15). Days of sore trial; yet no doubt days of spiritual and physical rest and refreshment.

Carriages. Old Saxon way of describing baggage.

GREAT EXPERIENCES

In these verses we have at least seven different and tumultuous experiences of the Apostle Paul

I. A GREAT WELCOME 21. 17-19
He merited this hearty welcome so warmly given, first by the general body of believers (17), then next day by the elders (18).

II. A GREAT CONCESSION 21. 20-26
Was Paul in error in following the advice of the elders ? Many think so. But the stronger a man's faith, the greater will be and should be his disposition to conciliate. Paul's objection was not to the ceremonial, but on the insistence of it as necessary to salvation. " He knew that the death-warrant of Jewish ceremonial had been signed, but he could leave it to time to carry out the sentence."

III. A GREAT TUMULT 21. 27-40
Observe the calmness of Paul. Remembering he was a Jew, there is nothing more striking than his self-command and composure in all circumstances.

IV. A GREAT LIGHT 22. 1-6
Paul's address to the angry mob is a rare example of skilful and conciliatory oratory. He gave his personal testimony.

V. A GREAT REBUKE 22. 7, 8
What a rebuke the Lord gave to Saul ! How quick he was to recognise it and respond.

VI. A GREAT CALL 22. 9-13
Called of the Lord, yet final and detailed directions were left to a humble servant of the Master. How He honours His servants.

VII. A GREAT COMMISSION 22. 14, 15
How welcome this message must have been after three days of darkness and solitude.

Was Paul Wrong ? The suggestion was a compromise between the Jewish believers and Paul. Compromises are always delicate, often difficult, and sometimes dangerous, and are only justifiable if there is no sacrifice of principle. This compromise did not serve its purpose, but rather the opposite, bringing the apostle into a false position. Even the advice of elders and of a majority may be wrong. We cannot dogmatise, but we can learn the lessons.

1. *If Paul was right*—then how difficult it is to break down prejudice, especially religious prejudice ; and we must be willing to submit to anything if the Gospel is to be furthered.

Continued on page 123

CHOSEN

What a great word is this! It is of supreme importance.
Though a simple word, yet when the choice is of God
how broad, how deep, and how full of meaning.

I. ITS IMPORTANCE : means **Salvation** ..   Eph. 1. 4
How vital to a company of passengers on a sinking
ship with but limited boat accommodation. How
vital to an applicant for a situation if he has depen-
dents. Am I chosen of God ? Our lifeboat, the Lord
Jesus, is able to save all.

II. ITS HONOUR : means **Service**
Like a soldier chosen for a perilous task, Saul was
chosen for service as well as salvation.

III. ITS DATE : means **Comfort**   ..   ..   Eph. 1. 4
From all eternity, in His everlasting purpose and
decrees. God chooses such as He foreknew would
believe.

IV. ITS SPHERE : means **Honouring Christ**   Eph. 1. 4
" In Him." To bear His image and glorify Him by
the beauty and saintliness of Christian life.

V. ITS COMFORT : means **Edification**
The knowledge of these facts is wonderfully strengthening.

VI. ITS END : means **Privilege**   ..   ..   verses 14, 15
1. **Know**—His Will.
2. **See**—His Face.
3. **Hear**—His Voice.
4. **Live**—in His Presence and as He wishes.
5. **Tell**—His Story.

VII. ITS MYSTERY : means **Worship**   ..   Rev. 17. 14
How am I to know I am chosen ? How can I penetrate
into the secret counsels of God ? This should not
concern us till we have responded to His call.

" **See that Just One** " (verse 14). " Just One " was one of the Jewish
names of Messiah.

Another Rendering. Instead of " Chosen " (W. and 20 C.), give " Appointed."

Claiming our Rights. Evidently by verses 25 to 30 we see there are
times when we can claim our civic and national rights.

CONSCIENCE

I. EVIL	Heb. 10. 22
II. AWAKENED	John 8. 9 ; Rom. 2. 15
III. PURGED	Heb. 9. 14
IV. GOOD	Acts 23. 1
V. SENSITIVE	2 Cor. 4. 2
VI. WEAK	1 Cor. 8. 7
VII. DEFILED	Titus 1. 15
VIII. SEARED	1 Tim. 4. 2

Paul and Conscience. What a man he was for conscience. The word occurs more than 30 times in the New Testament, and of these more than 20 are in Paul's writings.

Paul's Habit. He often appeals to his conscientiousness as the habit of his life (Rom. 9. 1), and even before his conversion (Acts 26. 9 ; Phil. 3. 5 and 6). To Ananias (verse 2), this assertion of a life so utterly unlike his own, seemed almost like a personal insult. He fitted the cap, and raged with a brutal cruelty.

Cruel Blow (verse 3). This cruel blow proved that no fair trial would be granted, so Paul adroitly used the people's animosities to end the meeting.

Prophecy. Verse 3 was really a prophecy terribly fulfilled by his murder in the Siege of Jerusalem.

" I wist not " (verse 5). Ananias had not been legally elected to that position. Then Paul had been long absent from Jerusalem.

GOOD CHEER

There are Five Essentials to a life of Good Cheer.

I. SINS FORGIVEN ..   ..   Matt. 9. 2

The consciousness of sins forgiven. Respected by his neighbours, yet in grave spiritual peril. He thought only of bodily needs.

II. UNION WITH GOD   ..   ..   ..   Matt. 9. 22

She had come into saving touch with Jesus Christ. The Master compelled confession to secure the attachment of the healed to the Healer. " Thy faith " not " fingers," symbolising union of the soul with God through the Lord Jesus Christ.

III. FELLOWSHIP WITH CHRIST ..   ..   Matt. 14. 27

They felt deserted out at night in a storm. When HE comes the MORNING comes. He cheers by His presence.

IV. INDWELLING OF THE LORD ..   ..   John 16. 33

Strangest of all His " good cheers," spoken on the way to Gethsemane, and only a few hours before Calvary. He, the Conqueror, will come and abide within.

V. COMMUNION WITH THE LORD   ..   Acts 23. 11

Night following a day of strife and confusion. It is always refreshing to have quiet after tumult. But there was something which made this solitude unwelcome, a slip, an unwise retort. This visit meant forgiveness for deviation, commendation for the testimony he had given, and assurance concerning his life and work. Times of retirement are essential for the life of good cheer. See what natural means were devised by God for the preservation of Paul (12-35).

Our Lord's Cheering Ministry. Our Lord exercised a welcome ministry of good cheer. When He desired to cheer a sad heart He used a word which can be either translated Cheer or Courage.

A Reason. He never urged people to " cheer up," without giving them a good reason for so doing.

How is Such a Life Possible ? " It is largely a matter of temperament, environment, and habit," many say. True, some are naturally of a sanguine disposition, whilst others cultivate this happy and useful habit. But there is something else. A Christian woman moved into a new flat, which had rather a dreary outlook. Calling to see her, this cheerful housewife invited her guest to note the pleasant outlook from her window. " Yes," was the reply of the visitor, " I see a remarkably fine lot of chimneys and back buildings." " Chimneys and back buildings," exclaimed the hostess, " Why, I never saw them before. I looked over all that you

Continued on page 123

PAUL'S CONSCIENCE

Paul's aim was to have an unoffending conscience (verse 16). Why ? " Herein," *i.e.*, in this belief. It was the practical result of his faith in the doctrine of the resurrection, Divine truth applied to daily living. How came this ?

I. ENLIGHTENMENT .. .. .. 1 Tim. 1. 9

Conscience is not an infallible guide. It requires illuminating, enlightening.

II. OBEDIENCE

If an alarm clock is not at first obeyed, it will ultimately cease to arouse, though it rings as loud as usual.

III. SHARPENING

As a sythe requires repeated sharpening, so conscience requires the daily application of the Word of God.

IV. TUNING

Pianos require regular tuning, so conscience needs to be tuned by regular prayer.

V. GUARDING

Exotic plants require to be guarded. Conscience is a tender exotic plant from Heaven.

VI. PURIFYING

By the precious Blood of Christ.

Providence (verse 2). The tendency to clothe the Roman Emperors with divine attributes led to the use of the phrase " providence of Caesar " on their coins and medals. Tertullus goes one step further, and extends the term to the Governor of Judaea.

Cheerfully (verse 10). Not with pale face and trembling fear, for he had nothing to be ashamed of.

To Worship (verse 11). One who had come to worship was not likely to profane.

" Exercise " (verse 16). The word is remarkable. It is a term applied elsewhere to the training of an athlete. It expresses the long course of discipline by which alone a man could be prepared for a gymnastic feat.

A GREAT SERMON

In Paul's addresses we see some of the secrets of a great sermon

I. LOGICAL .. .. verse 25
   He " reasoned," he was not dogmatic, but gave proof.

II. PERSONAL .. .. verse 25
   He did not beat about the bush, but applied the truth to Felix.

III. PRACTICAL .. .. verse 25
   It dealt with facts of life, not airy somethings and nothings.

IV. COURAGEOUS .. .. verse 25
   No faltering. He hit the nail on the head, calling a spade a spade.

V. DOCTRINAL .. .. verse 25
   1. **Righteousness.** " Justice " (w.). The giving to all their due, the fulfilling of every relation in which we stand to others. The life the Law of God demands we are unable to render. Then, the righteousness by faith.

   2. **Temperance.** Intemperance degrades. It levels man to the beasts. Temperance is the holding of the reins of conduct in the hand of will.

   3. **Judgment to Come.** The Great White Throne for all the unsaved, the Judgment Seat of Christ for the rewarding of believers.

VI. SCRIPTURAL .. .. verse 24
   About Christ. " The faith in Christ."

VII. POWERFUL .. .. verse 25
   So mighty that Felix trembled.

Strange Audience. What a strange audience had Paul. Felix, a man of servile birth, who, with his brother, had been favourite slaves of the Emperor, and had both risen to high position. Tacitus describes him as wielding kingly power with the disposition of a slave, disgracing it by all manner of cruelty and lust. Drusilla, youngest daughter of the Herod of Acts 12. 1. She was aged 6 when her father died. At 15 she married King Emesa. Felix persuaded her, through the Simon Magus of Acts 8. 9 to 25, to leave her husband and live with him. She and her son by Felix perished in the great eruption of Vesuvius which overthrew Pompeii and Herculaneum.

The Silent Two Years. Two years passed between verses 26 and 27. The Gospel of Luke is said to have been written by Luke under the guidance of Paul at this time.

Paul and Felix. What a contrast. Felix was physically free, but how

Continued on page 124

PROCRASTINATION

Felix waited for a "convenient season." Why do people
procrastinate ?

I. APPEARANCE

It seems courteous and honourable. It does not look
like a refusal but a postponement, and that seems
respectable. But it is not what it seems to be.

II. CONVENIENCE

It is an easy way to lull to sleep an awakened conscience.
It is inconvenient to feel miserable. It looks like a
courteous way to get rid of a Christian worker.

III. CONSCIENCE

It is an easy way to get rid of a disagreeable subject,
e.g., "righteousness, temperance, judgment " (verse
25).

IV. NEGLIGENCE

It is a common but mistaken idea, that there is **time
enough yet** to think about serious things.

Lost Soul. This was how Felix, the Roman Governor, lost his soul.
Awakened by the faithful and powerful preaching of the Gospel, he lulled
his frightened heart and conscience to sleep by procrastination.

Contrast. What contrasts we have here. Felix trembled as the Word
of the Lord laid hold of him. Conscience was God's ally in that man's
life, and its warning bell rang loudly. Drusilla, his partner in sin, seemed
unimpressed. *She* was not alarmed. Perhaps she was too frivolous.

A Bad Habit of Felix. It seemed to be one of Felix's bad habits. He
procrastinated in his duty as Governor in respect to Paul. Felix had
"perfect knowledge of that way " (verse 22), and there was only one
righteous course for him to do, discharge this prisoner. The reason he
gave for not doing so was merely an excuse (verse 26).

"Now." Dr. Pierson has stated : "No sinner ever finds a convenient
season. That is my deep conviction. What is a convenient season ?
A season when it will be agreeable and easy to turn to God. In the nature
of the case it is never easy to abandon sin, never easy to turn from evil to
good, never a convenient time to revolutionise life. If you want a convenient season it is your most convenient season now."

ALMOST PERSUADED

Was the king sincere or sarcastic ? Did he speak in irony or in earnest ? Felix was evasive as well as derisive.

I. SARCASM

" **You make a mistake if you think you can so easily persuade me to be a Christian** ! " This is the view of those who think he spoke in derision.

1. It will require more than this to make me a Christian !

2. You need not think that I, like you, will become a Christian so suddenly and easily (Paul had been giving his testimony, showing how suddenly he was converted).

3. You seem to think that, with a little effort, you can make so great a man as I am, a Christian ! You are mistaken.

4. It was a piece of sarcastic contempt.

5. He is half amused and half angry at the apostle's presumption.

II. SERIOUSNESS

" **You have almost persuaded me to become a Christian.** " Is there behind the scorn some apprehension ? Did he feel himself weakening before Paul's message, and was he endeavouring to conceal inward emotion under a show of pleasantry. "Almost—but lost ! "

Entertainment. Felix kept Paul two years in prison. Then Festus succeeded him. The trial under Festus convinced Paul that he would not meet with justice under him, so appealed to Caesar (25. 10 and 11). Agrippa and his sister came to salute Festus. The festivities had been going on for several days when Festus, bethinking him of his prisoner, thought of a novel idea of entertainment, and had him before them.

Courtesy. Note Paul's courtesy—he was silent till liberty to speak was given (26. 1), and answered sarcasm (verse 28) by earnest entreaty (verse 29).

What Roused Festus ? The statement that the despised Nazarene, crucified under Pontius Pilate, should give light to the Gentiles (26. 23). Now the prisoner is lost in the evangelist (25 to 27).

A FAVORABLE WIND

What folly it is to reject good advice, as this Centurion did

I. PRUDENCE BEFORE PROVIDENCE

"Those know not their danger who choose to be governed more by human prudence than by Divine revelation," are the words of an old writer.

II. REJECTING GOOD ADVICE

The world is wise if it does not reject the good advice given by the godly (verse 11).

III. CIVILITY INSUFFICIENT

Civility to God's servants is not sufficient. The Centurion was very civil to Paul, yet rejected his advice.

IV. TRUE WISDOM

It is wiser to hearken to Heaven than to earthly experts.

"**Supposing**" (verse 13). What a word this is ! But they were mistaken. Have you ever studied the suppositions of the Bible ?

(a) Taking His Presence for granted (Luke 2. 24).

(b) Taking Him for less than He was (John 20. 15).

(c) The World taking for granted that God's people will do as others (Acts 16. 27).

(d) Supposing the Lord to be what He was not (Luke 24. 3).

South Wind. It is not always a proof that we are doing right when a favourable wind blows.

Luke was evidently with Paul, as indicated by the " we " (27. 1).

Inspiring Confidence (verse 3). Here is Paul still inspiring confidence. "His look was his certificate ; his tone was his letter of recommendation."

"**Refresh**" (verse 3). Every meeting with fellow-believers should be refreshing.

"**Hardly Passing**" (verse 8). Coasting along with difficulty.

"**Much time was spent**" (9). Waited 25 days, from Sept. 1 to 25.

"**Fast**" (verse 9). The Fast of the great Day of Atonement.

"**Perceive**" (verse 10). Paul knew this either by (1) revelation from God, or (2) from his own knowledge gained by long experience. He had been shipwrecked thrice (2 Cor. 11), and on one of these occasions had floated a day and a night on the deep.

FRUITS OF FAITH

Some of the fruits that follow faith in God

I. **DELIVERANCE**

Deliverance from the guilt of sin. Faith, *not* tears (Rom. 5. 1).

II. **RIGHTEOUSNESS**

A change of life. Since he believed God, his life had been completely changed.

III. **CONFESSION**

It is our duty to boldly confess Him by lip as well as life.

IV. **ASSURANCE**

He who gives himself to God, gets God for himself.

V. **UPLIFT**

Uplifted above the petty meannesses of life. A less noble nature would have said more in vindication of the wisdom of his former advice (verse 21) or have sulked.

VI. **CALMNESS**

Paul stands forth with calm and confidence, and inspires them all with new hope and good cheer.

"**I Believe God**" (verse 25). Not, I believe in a God. There is a great difference between these two short sentences. It is good when we can say, "I believe in a God." But the devils go so far (James 2. 19). They "believe and tremble," literally "shudder," and that is more than some men do.

Events. The ship was helplessly driven before the wind (verse 15). "They" (verse 17) were the crew; "we" (18 and 19), crew and passengers. These were the last attempts to save themselves. "All hope...was taken away." Idleness breeds despair.

Good Cheer. In the midst of that gloomy company was one who prayed and got the answer ("hath given thee," verse 24—then he must have asked for them). What a miraculous change passes on externals when faith looks at them!

GRACE BEFORE MEAT

The offering of thanks to God before partaking food is to the Christian—

I. A DUTY

1. **Common Gratitude** demands it. Charles Lamb thought he could trace the origin of saying grace to natural gratitude in days of the hunt, when a good meal was a rare and uncertain boon. It certainly was the habit of Israel from ancient times.

2. **Following Christ's Example**, who always gave thanks, and in some peculiar way that by this act he was recognised at Emmaus (Luke 24. 30, 31). The habit is at once so natural and so seemly that the extent to which it is not practised is a matter for wonder, indignation, and regret.

II. A CONFESSION .. .. verse 35

Sometimes this is a young convert's first confession of Christ before relatives or friends.

III. AN EDUCATION

Cultivating a habit of thanksgiving, and is thus a daily education.

IV. AN ACT OF CONSECRATION .. .. 1 Tim. 4, 5

Something does happen when we ask a blessing.

V. A REMINDER

Of our indebtedness to and dependence upon God for all good gifts for both body and soul.

" **And when he had thus spoken** " (verse 35). Here is precept and example ; good advice given by one who practised it. And thus it had the desired effect—others followed his example.

Night Time. " Fourteenth night " (verse 27). Night, with its terrors, fears, and alarms, with its darkness and gloom. But God gave Paul songs in the night.

Sound Common Sense. There was sound commonsense in the advice. He knew that the moment for intense struggle was at hand, and so he prepares them for it by persuading them to eat a substantial meal. Thus exhausted nature was refreshed.

Grace Before Meat. Paul shows them by example (verse 35) how a Christian partakes of food. He said grace publicly, but not for show. It was his regular habit.

" **Mair shame to you, sir.** " In a Scottish parish lived a dear old Scottish woman, who for many years kept house for the bachelor minister. On one occasion it happened that, in the absence of the minister, several gentlemen were partaking of luncheon in the manse. The soup was brought in and laid down by Margaret, who then stood behind the chair at the head of the table. A pause ensued, and at last the occupant of the chair said " Margaret, remove the cover." " Ask the blessing first, sir," she said,

Continued on page 124

PAUL AT MALTA

I. RECIPIENT OF DIVINE FAVOUR .. .. verse 1

How different is the kindness of the Lord ! Shown while in the midst of the waves. A kindness that plunges in to save, not standing on shore and watching.

II. SHARER OF HUMAN KINDNESS .. .. verse 2

When God brings to shore He does not leave us there to care for ourselves. We are the continued objects of His tender care. He causes others to be kind to us.

III. CONSIDERATE AND UNSELFISH .. .. verse 3

Paul is still thinking of others, not absorbed in his own needs. Note his carefulness, "*laid* them on the fire," did not pitch them. Even this humble service was not unbecoming.

IV. OBJECT OF DIVINE CARE .. .. verses 3-6

Though bitten, God protected him. Note the rash judgment (verse 6).

V. MEDIUM OF BLESSING .. .. verses 7-10

1. The chief man's courtesy (7).
2. His trouble at home (8).
3. Paul's unsolicited prayer and its result.

" **All.**" " And so it came to pass that they escaped *all* safe to land " (27. 44). And it always does to a trusting soul. That 276 men on a wreck, many of whom were unable to swim, should *all* be saved, was most im-probable. Yet it was God's promise (27. 24).

" **Where are we ?** " That was the first question of the saved, so com-pletely had they lost their reckoning. Soon they discovered they were on Malta.

" **How shall we be received ?** " That would be their second question. They were wet, cold, weary, anxious, huddled together on the shore in the early morning. No ordinary kindness was shown them. " Because of the *pelting* rain " (W.).

" **When they were escaped, then they knew** " (verse 1). We cannot know our sins are forgiven until we are saved.

HUMAN SYMPATHY

Here is an illustration of the power of human sympathy. Their presence cheered Paul, because it gave him a threefold proof regarding the Church at Rome.

I. THEIR LOYALTY TO GOD

In spite of persecutions. Each disciple in those days had to pass through a fiery baptism. Such experience had a winnowing effect. Would *they* endure ? Yes. Their presence was a proof of their patient endurance.

II. THEIR LOYALTY TO PAUL

In spite of Paul's altered position, they were not ashamed to meet him, nor afraid to stand by him. Paul loved company. But he was now a prisoner. Would they be ashamed of him ? Their coming said " No ! "

III. THEIR FELLOWSHIP

Their coming to meet him was also proof that the Church received him heartily in the Lord.

At Sea Again. They spent three months at Malta. A ship had wintered there. They took berths in her.

Castor and Pollux (verse 11). The twin brethren, the patrons of sailors. Their images were displayed on the bow of the boat.

Land at Last. At last they completed their voyage. At the sea port they found brethren, and were allowed to spend seven days with them (verse 14).

News at Rome. These seven days gave messengers time to acquaint the Church at Rome of Paul's landing. A deputation was sent to meet him.

Deputation. From Puteoli to Rome was a march of 140 miles. The deputation had travelled 30 miles, when they rested at The Three Taverns, save for a few who were so eager they pushed on ten miles farther to Appii Forum.

At last they met, first those who pushed on, then later the others. And their presence had a wonderful effect upon the missionary.

Was he Depressed ? It seems so. But their presence cheered him. Why ? (See above outline.)

ROME AT LAST

" So we came to Rome " (verse 14, R.V.)

I. PLANS THWARTED

It is possible for God to thwart our plans, and yet grant our desire. How different was this coming to Rome to the one Paul must have thought of !

II. PRAYERS REFUSED

It is possible for God to refuse our prayers and yet grant our desires (compare Romans 1. 14).

III. HIS TRUST

Are we, like Paul, willing to trust the details of our programmes to the Lord ?

Why Treated Kindly ? Probably through the kind intervention of the Centurion, who had conceived a sincere admiration for him during their months of travel together, that Paul, on reaching Rome, found himself treated with great leniency. He was allowed to have a private house or apartment in the neighbourhood of the Prætorian barracks.

Captain of the Guard (of verse 16) was Burrhus, a famous soldier of high character and great influence.

His Great Desire, long cherished, was to preach the Gospel in Rome (Rom. 1. 14). But he little dreamt in what strange ways God would grant his desire. " We too are often surprised at the shape which God's answers to our wishes take. Well for us if we take the unexpected or painful events which accomplish some long-cherished purpose as cheerfully and boldly as did Paul."

Work Amongst Soldiers. During that two years Paul did a great work amongst the Roman soldiers. History informs us that this was the beginning of a movement, destined within three centuries, to permeate the entire army, and compel Constantine to adopt Christianity as the religion of the State.

PREACHING IN ROME

I. TO THE JEW FIRST .. .. .. verse 17-24

1. **His Urgency.** No time lost (verse 17). After such a voyage, many less eager would have required several weeks of rest. He only took three days.
2. **His Innocency** (verse 17).
3. **His Good Feeling towards his own nation** (verse 19).
4. **His Conviction.** "What thou *thinkest*" (verse 22). As if the matter in hand was only a matter of opinions.
5. **His Patience.** A whole day reasoning and exhorting (23 and 24).

II. TO THE GENTILES .. .. .. verses 25-31

1. **Jewish Official Rejection** (verse 25).
2. **Foretold** (verses 26 and 27). What a strange and tragic scene this final leave-taking was between Paul and the leader of the Rome Jewry.
3. **Two Years' Gospel Ministry which Extolled the Lord Jesus Christ** (verse 31).

Jews in Rome. It has been computed that there were then 60,000 Jews in Rome, the general objects of dislike and ridicule. What a field for Christian enterprise.

Why the Two Years' Delay? Perhaps partly due to give Paul's accusers time to prepare their case and travel to the Imperial City; but probably mainly due to the Emperor's shameless indulgence which he allowed to interfere with his discharge of public business.

Paul's Subsequent History.

A.D. 61. Arrival in Rome, two years a prisoner.

,, 62. (About end.) Wrote Ephesians, Philippians, Colossians, Philemon.

,, 63. Release and free for about four years, visiting Asia Minor and Macedonia again, and also going to Spain. Probably wrote 1 Tim. and Titus during the latter part of this time.

,, 68. Rearrested, taken to Rome, and wrote 2 Tim. Two trials and martyrdom.

Continued from page 54

(d) *Imprisonments in Rome* (28. 16-31)

Note, they arrived in Rome, A.D. 61, and Paul remained two years. At end of A.D. 62 he wrote Ephesians, Philippians, Colossians, and Philemon. Released from A.D. 63-67, visiting Asia Minor, Macedonia, and Spain. Re-arrested in A.D. 68 and again taken to Rome. Wrote 1 and 2 Timothy and Titus. After two trials was put to death.

Continued from page 55

tian teaching is vain is the indifference and non-expectant attitude of the hearers.

Peter's Lodgings. Whilst at Joppa Peter lodged with a namesake of his, only one engaged in an unclean trade according to Jewish opinions. Very remarkable that Peter should stay there !

Caesarea was the Roman Capital of Palestine. Very remarkable that Philip was there (Acts 8. 40), yet Cornelius not directed to send for him.

Was Cornelius a Saved Man ? Not in the Gospel sense (11. 14). It is evident he was a Jewish proselyte. See how far one can go and yet not be right with God.

" **Peter went with them** " (verse 23). It took Peter and others years to digest the lesson given on the house-top, though he began to put it into practice that day.

Continued from page 56

thing, a verbal luxury. The putting into a parenthesis this great truth by our grammarians and printers is significant of the view many take of Him. Thousands neither recognise Him as Saviour or Lord. Many want His salvation, but do not care to recognise His Lordship over the saved soul. A full salvation can never be enjoyed without a full recognition of this. Is He Lord of all your being, of your time and talents? Crown Him Lord of all !

The Result (44-48). For the first time the Holy Spirit descended on a Gentile gathering who had received the same Gospel as the Jews on the Day of Pentecost, Peter using the key to open the door to the Gentiles.

Continued from page 58

and the people of Antioch were puzzled about this new sect. They could not make them out. So they invented a new name for them—Christians.

Genius of Antioch. Curiously we learn from the Emperor Julian that the people of Antioch in his day had a tendency and genius for the invention of nick-names.

Hybrid. Philologically, it is a hybrid word—Christ is Greek ; the termination " ian," Latin, meaning adherent, follower, partisan. Observe this name originated not with their Jewish enemies, but with the heathen in Antioch.

Various Names. The above outlines suggest a brief study of the names by which the primitive Christians were known in the order in which they occur. The name Christian was the last. The proposition is that, to be worthy of that name, we must be worthy of bearing all the others.

Continued from page 61

History.   The apostle's accuser was so impressed by his good confession before his judges, that he there and then declared himself a believer, and was condemned to die with him.   On the way to execution, he begged forgiveness of James, who replied, " Peace be unto thee ! " and kissed him. And they were beheaded together.

A Fatal Policy.   To act only to please others (verse 3) is a fatal policy. Josephus states that Herod liked peace (note verses 21 and 22).

Foolish !   What is the use of prayer on this occasion ?   It may seem foolish, but unarmed hands lifted in prayer wield a mightier weapon than sword, spear, or gun.   Let us note the prayer that moves.

Continued from page 72

> profitless, he sends for now as being profitable.
> What an honour to be asked for by the dying.
> 3. And John Mark was now ready to stand by Paul's
>   side in Rome at the risk of imprisonment and of
>   death.   Christ can lay hold of the veriest coward and
>   make him a lion.

Much in Little.   All that the New Testament has to say about Mark is found in but a few verses.   But how significant !   What a fruitful study they make.

Not Unimportant.   This is no unimportant study, for Mark wrote the Gospel that bears his name.

Continued from page 77

would have thought that, after all they had endured, that Paul and Silas would themselves have needed comfort.   What unselfishness !

Sunrises.   There is a great difference between a sunrise in the tropics and the arctics.   " Some have a spiritual sunrise as in the tropics, where the one moment is grey and cold, and the next moment the earth and sea are lit with glory.   Others have a sunrise as at the Poles, where a long, slowly growing light precedes the rising, and the rising is scarcely observable."

Continued from page 80

> 4. **A Life of Praise** requires Bible Searching (Psa. 119.
>   171).   Ability to praise God is proportionate to
>   understanding of God's statutes.

A Chinese scholar for the first time saw and came into possession of a copy of the Bible.   Though he knew nothing of the Christian religion, the reading of the Book made a tremendous impression upon him.   To a missionary he exclaimed : *"The one who made that Book made me."*   He was convinced that it was the product of something infinitely surpassing the highest human genius.

Thessalonica.   After the stirring events of chapter 16, Paul and his companion continued their itinerary through Amphipolis and Apollonia to Thessalonica.

" **As his manner was** " (verse 2) he began his labours in the Synagogue, ministering there three Sabbath days. Results were cheering. *Some* Jews "believed," but of the "Greeks a great multitude," with a number of high-born ladies (verse 4).

For "**Lewd Fellows**" W. gives "idle rascals."

Encouraging Testimony. What a wonderfully encouraging testimony to the power of the Christian Gospel we have in verse 6.

True Nobility. What true nobleness is, and how it manifests itself, according to God's estimate, is in verse 11 disclosed by God the Holy Ghost.

Continued from page 85

2. Not ourselves (2 Cor. 4. 5). This can be done by tone as well as by the words we use.

3. The Gospel (Mark 16. 15), *i.e.*, Christ's Gospel (2 Cor. 2. 12).

4. Not man's conception of the Gospel (Gal. 1. 11). Forget not the "woes" (1 Cor. 9. 16 ; Gal. 1. 8, 9).

5. What is the Gospel ? The Death of Christ (1 Cor. 15. 3) by Crucifixion (1 Cor. 1. 23).

This Subject is continued in the next Study.

Continued from page 87

(Rom. 3. 12. "Have turned worthless" is W. rendering.

(*b*) Though unprofitable, man is still valued by God (see above outline).

(*c*) Though unprofitable, we can through transforming grace become profitable to God (Philemon 11).

Continued from page 106

2. *If Paul was Wrong*—what comfort it is to us. Even the great apostle making mistakes, and yet afterwards, his sweetest writings flow from his pen. How great is the grace that can restore and use even those who err.

A Mad Rush. A close study of verse 35 shows us that as the crowd saw their captives escaping, they made one last fierce mad rush, and almost swept away the soldiers who had to pick Paul up and carry him off for safety.

Continued from page 109

see and saw those magnificent trees which form such a picturesque line on the horizon. I thought only of the trees, and the glorious sunsets I see from this window." Yet something else is required.

A Mosaic. This word of cheer no doubt was often on our Lord's lips, but only five occurrences are preserved. These five make a beautiful mosaic. Put together they show us what is required to make our life buoyant, bold, cheerful, courageous—a life with wings.

124 Outline Studies in Acts

Continued from page 111

terribly bound. Paul was a prisoner, but the real free man of the two.
Paul was cheerful (verse 10), Felix trembled (verse 25).

Paul's Subject Matter (verse 25). 1, *Man and his past.* " Righteousness " needed because of sin, provided in the sacrifice of Christ, imputed
because of faith. 2, *Man and the present.* " Temperance," *i.e.*, in all
things. 3, *Man and the future.* " Judgment to come." For those unsaved,
condemnation for rejecting Christ. For the saved, works judged and
rewarded or burnt.

Continued from page 116

respectfully. " The truth is," confessed the gentleman, after a moment's
deliberation, " that it is so long since I said it that I have forgotten how
to." The reply was sharp and pertinent. " Mair shame to you, sir."

" **From God.** " The story goes that a man met a boy on a country road
with a basket of bread on his arm. " What have you got in that basket,
my boy ? " asked the man. " Bread, sir." " Where did you get that
bread ? " " From the baker, sir." " And where did the baker get it
from ? " " He made it of flour." " And where did he get the flour from ? "
" From the farmer, sir." " And where did the farmer get the flour from ? "
" From seed, sir." " And where did he get the seed from ? " The boy
paused, then exclaimed in an awe-struck voice, " From God, sir ! " Yes,
behind each of those loaves was God ! " The eyes of all look (*margin*)
unto Thee ; and Thou givest them their meat in due season," says the
Psalmist. " Thou openest Thine hand and satisfiest the desire of every
living thing." We breathe God's air every day, and use the limbs God
has given us, and eat God's food, and yet how many people ever look up
and give thanks.

Other Sermon Outline Titles Available:

Briggs, S.R. and Elliot, J.H.
  600 BIBLE GEMS AND OUTLINES

Jabez Burns Sermon Outline Series
  149 SERMON OUTLINES
  151 SERMON OUTLINES
  199 SERMON OUTLINES
  200 SERMON OUTLINES
  201 SERMON OUTLINES
   91 SERMON OUTLINES ON TYPES
      AND METAPHORS

Marsh, F.E.
   500 BIBLE STUDY OUTLINES
  1000 BIBLE STUDY OUTLINES
  ILLUSTRATED BIBLE STUDY OUTLINES

John Ritchie Sermon Outline Series
  500 SERMON OUTLINES ON BASIC
      BIBLE TRUTHS
  500 CHILDREN'S SERMON OUTLINES
  500 EVANGELISTIC SERMON OUTLINES
  500 GOSPEL ILLUSTRATIONS
  500 GOSPEL SERMON OUTLINES
  500 SERMON OUTLINES ON THE
      CHRISTIAN LIFE

Easy-to-Use Sermon Outline Series
Edited by Charles R. Wood
EVANGELISTIC SERMON OUTLINES
REVIVAL SERMON OUTLINES
SERMON OUTLINES FOR FUNERAL
   SERVICES
SERMON OUTLINES FOR SPECIAL DAYS
   AND OCCASIONS
SERMON OUTLINES FOR TEENS
SERMON OUTLINES FROM PROVERBS
SERMON OUTLINES FROM THE SERMON
   ON THE MOUNT
SERMON OUTLINES ON THE PSALMS